Foreword by
ORRIN WOODWARD

REVOLU-TIONARY LEAD-ERSHIP

OBSTACLES
PRESS

Life Leadership Essentials Series

First Edition, January 2016
10 9 8 7 6 5 4 3 2 1

Published by:
Obstaclés Press
200 Commonwealth Court
Cary, NC 27511

lifeleadership.com

ISBN 978-0-9970293-8-3

Cover design and layout by Norm Williams, nwa-inc.com

Printed in the United States of America

"Leadership is diving for the loose ball...."
— LARRY BIRD

CONTENTS

FOREWORD

Vision is tomorrow's reality expressed as an idea to-day, and leaders are the people who make these expressions a reality. The book you hold in your hands contains five of the most influential revolutionary leaders in the history of humanity. More personally, each of these leaders/thinkers has influenced my life and helped me understand the journey from ideas to implementation.

One of my favorite quotes is, "When all is said and done, much more is said than ever done." Each of us knows the truth of this statement first hand, especially if the reader was subjected to endless corporate meetings that discussed the same issues month after month without changing anything of substance. Interestingly, reading the lives of revolutionary leaders was what helped me make the leap from corporate America into entrepreneurial enterprises. I simply needed to know whether I had what it takes to become successful in the marketplace.

Indeed, when I read books about Benjamin Franklin, who started with nothing but hunger and guts and yet became one of the most refined renaissance men in American history, I was inspired. In the same era as

Franklin, another man refused to back down to tyranny and oppression. That is why everyone remembers Patrick Henry and his famous *Give Me Liberty of Give Me Death* speech. One final member of the trinity of leaders from the founding generation of America is Andrew Jackson, who took on the financial elites of his generation and won. Each of these three men was self-educated and formed his sterling character through the trials and turmoil of life.

The final two revolutionary leaders studied come from the modern era. The first created the largest retailing empire in the world through vision, drive, and humility. Sam Walton, despite taking on billion-dollar giants entering the discount store model, refused to lose. Through an ingenious model of duplication and a world-class leadership culture built around Walton's never-ending hunger to improve, Wal-Mart grew through every challenge. Personally, I believe Sam Walton was the greatest leader of the twentieth century.

Finally, the last member of this select company is a revolutionary leader because he captured what made revolutionary leaders different from the rest of us and wrote numerous books on the subject. Peter Drucker's self-education model was second to none. In fact, every year he would pick a subject that interested him and deep-dive into it by reading twenty, fifty, sometimes over a hundred books on the subject. He started this unique habit early in life and was still going strong into his 90s! Imagine the level of education one can acquire if he or she wakes up every day with that level of specific intent. Drucker was one of the driving forces of the management revolution that changed the history of economic progress.

Although these revolutionary leaders were different in personality, temperament, and style, they also had many underlying similarities. For starters, each had a level of conviction that drove him forward despite incredible levels of resistance from the powers-that-be. Remember, every person who wants to change the world meets resistance from the current powers, who want to keep the world the same. Another similarity: each revolutionary leader had a vision that he didn't just talk about; rather, he spent his whole life acting upon it. Great leaders model before they message, and these leaders never asked others to do what they were not willing to do themselves.

Finally, these revolutionary leaders never sold out their convictions for their convenience. To be sure, the higher you climb the mountain of success, the more comfortable camping spots you will find. However, once a person starts camping, his/her ability to make a difference is severely compromised. These leaders knew what they wanted to accomplish, moved in the direction of their dreams, and didn't stop progressing until they drew their last breath. In our age of image over integrity, this type of revolutionary leadership is desperately needed.

Read the book, ponder its lessons, and who knows, perhaps like Esther of old, the reader has been created for a time such as this.

Sincerely,

Orrin Woodward: *Inc. Magazine* Top 20 Leader; Guinness World Record Holder; and Chairman of the Board of LIFE Leadership

INTRODUCTION

*"Innovation distinguishes between
a leader and a follower."*
—STEVE JOBS

"We have it in our power to begin the world over again."
—THOMAS PAINE

T he world needs more leaders. Moreover, it needs a special kind of leader, the kind who envisions great improvements and knows—or figures out—how to bring them into reality. These are the revolutionary, the reformer, the innovator, the rebel, the visionary, and what best-selling author Chris Brady calls "rascals." These are a central and vital part of true leadership. And those who want to be leaders need to develop these traits.

Author Anais Nin claimed that "Societies in decline have no use for visionaries," meaning that such societies prefer not to have great leaders and often go to great lengths to discourage, discount, distract, and thwart those who do arise.

> **Nations in decline obviously feel some kind of major disconnect with vision.**

Yet declining societies also have the greatest use for vision-aries, because they need them more than any other type of people.

Nations in decline obviously feel some kind of major disconnect with vision. Maybe they have the wrong vision, or maybe they have a good one and don't follow it very well, or perhaps they have no vision at all. Often they simply lack leadership. Whatever the case, find a declining society, and you've found a society that has not only a great *use* but a deep *need* for more than a few powerful revolutionary leaders on every level.

Nevertheless, during such periods of decline, there remains a widespread lack of enthusiasm for change, innovation, ingenuity, initiative, progress, and leadership vision. Despite this fact — partially *because* of it — such leaders are desperately needed.

The Right Kind of Rebel

Even though they have to deal with the opposition and resistance of what seems like the whole world, there are visionary leaders today who stand up against stagnation, decline, and evil, even in times when doing so is both difficult and dangerous. These great

> **Even societies that are not in decline have a great need for such rebels and revolutionaries, producers and innovators.**

men and women are often called revolutionaries, or even rebels.

We aren't talking about teenage kids with extreme haircuts or students who insist on using their "outside" voices in the library. Rather, we mean revolutionaries like the members of the Underground Railroad during American slavery, and revolutionaries like the farmers, merchants, and others who put everything on the line to win American freedom during the Revolutionary War.

It is because of the vision, strength, wisdom, courage, tenacity, and virtue of such men and women that these eras of stagnancy, mediocrity, decline, and oppression ultimately ended and turned into times of freedom, prosperity, progress, and growth. Very Good!.

Without courageous and dedicated revolutionary leaders, decline would spread and society would end up somewhere drastically different.

Another Name for Visionary

Actually, even societies that are not in decline have a great need for such rebels and revolutionaries, producers and innovators. Times of great abundance and progress are generally characterized and led by visionaries just like these.

In fact, another name for visionary is *leader*, and leaders — great leaders, and lots of them — are needed in all societies and at all times in order for prosperity, freedom, excellence, and many other good things to exist and thrive in any civilization or group of people.

Revolutionary leader Thomas Jefferson said, "I hold it that a little rebellion now and then is a good thing, and as necessary in the political world as storms in the physical." In reality, this goes a step further: a little innovation in all fields is important now and then for growth.

Yet even for those in times of plenty, leadership isn't exactly a picnic. There are always enemies to excellence and innovation, skeptics, haters and critics who would rather tear things down than build or create anything themselves.

To put it bluntly, authentic leadership has never been an easy path, and there are always those who seek to put a stop to it in whatever ways they can manage. But leaders keep serving society anyway.

Even at the height of societal achievement, during a nation's golden age, genuine leadership is a revolution, since to truly be a leader you have to step up and add to or even shift the norm, which means going against it.

In this way, top leaders in all fields of endeavor and all epochs of history join the ranks of great revolutionary leaders.

Join the Club

Thus to the list of men and women like Joan of Arc, George Washington, Tecumseh, Frederick Douglass, and Gandhi, among others, we also add those like William Shakespeare, Marie Curie, Dale Carnegie, Mother Teresa, Buckminster Fuller, and Steve Jobs.

The list of revolutionary leaders in history, of individuals who have truly changed the world in meaningful and impactful ways, is certainly not limited to those we've mentioned or those we'll discuss in depth in the pages that follow. Yet sadly, they are greatly outnumbered by those who don't lead, who avoid revolutionary service. And as mentioned above, there are also some who seek to stand directly in their way and who support mediocrity even when great improvements are possible.

> **The world today has need of visionaries, and there have been many who lived before today whose words and examples are just *waiting* to mentor and guide those who wish to lead the next charge.**

Despite the difficulties and hardships involved in real leadership, the world, now and always, has great need for visionaries, revolutionaries, and dedicated leaders who are willing to stand up, make a change, and bring a positive difference to the world.

And, while leadership can be very challenging, it is also extremely rewarding for both the leaders and for those they effectively lead.

It isn't always easy to be excellent, but it is worth it. And in becoming a real leader, you are becoming a part of history's "A" Team, fighting in the age-old revolution for increased morality, prosperity, family values, success, and happiness. In essence, when you make the choice and take the steps necessary to become a true revolutionary leader, you are joining ranks and joining hands with those who have led the charge before you.

Simply put, if you're a revolutionary leader, you've got some of the most excellent, successful, and great men and women in history on your team. And if you're on their team, helping them with their cause, why not let them help you with yours?

Listen, Learn, Live

In this book, we'll introduce some of your most important and powerful teammates in the great battle for goodness and improvement and help you make the most of these partnerships.

> **To be a revolutionary leader, one must learn from what's been done before without assuming it's *all* been done.**

Top leaders understand that by learning from the greatest examples, lessons, stories, and words of those who have gone before, they are able to more fully achieve success on their own paths to greatness.

Everyone today has the opportunity to improve the world in incredible ways—to achieve great success and add unbelievable amounts of goodness, achievement, prosperity, happiness, and progress to their own lives and to the world. That's the great call to leadership. But we can't do these things unless we learn how.

The world today has need of revolutionary leaders, and there have been many who lived before today whose words and examples are just *waiting* to mentor and guide those of us who wish to lead the next charge in our generation.

These men and women didn't live silently, and their voices echo through to our world today. It's up to us to search out and listen to such voices, and to then learn from their teachings and to live accordingly.

It is easy to look back at those who have achieved success in the past and only see what they did and who they became, rather than understanding who they were before they reached the limelight, how they got their greatness, and what words of wisdom and secrets of success they have to share with those who wish to be great in our time.

> **If you're a revolutionary leader, you've got some of the most excellent, successful, and great men and women in history on your team.**

Today, more than ever, we need to be looking back at the heroes of the past and looking at the things they accomplished, the lessons they learned, and perhaps most importantly, the lessons they taught. We need leaders from all spheres of life to learn the great leadership teachings of those who went before and really achieved top-rate revolutionary leadership. Revolutionary leadership changes the world.

As Orrin Woodward taught, we need to be looking at their lives and the things they thought and understood and start to inculcate them back into our society today.

Effective leaders have long known that to get to the highest levels of achievement, it is extremely helpful (and at times essential) to emulate leaders who have already walked the path to such victories. Woodward has taught about the following five heroes as revolutionary leaders worthy of emulation:

Benjamin Franklin

Patrick Henry

Andrew Jackson

Peter Drucker

Sam Walton

Woodward has shared stories and lessons from the lives of these leaders in important speeches that are available on audio (more about this below). This book addresses the contributions of these five leaders even further, showing how their messages are incredibly relevant to anyone who wants to be a better, more effective leader today. We need to learn from each of them.

In fact, Woodward himself is an exemplary revolutionary leader. Thus, in the words and stories of these five great leaders and also the thoughts of Woodward about their unique contributions, we have six inspiring examples of revolutionary leadership. These leaders can help all of us on our own paths to success.

Be the Difference by Knowing the Sum

In short: revolutionary leaders aren't those who simply revolt against past generations. Rather, they stand on the shoulders of giants, don't attempt to reinvent the wheel, but also refuse to be held back by the accomplishments of others. New inventions are ahead. The wheel is wonderful, they realize, but the next level and the higher peak must be our focus.

To be a revolutionary leader, one must learn from what's been done before without assuming it's *all* been done.

Without truly knowing what's been achieved in the past by visionary leaders, learning from those advancements, and incorporating them into one's daily work and one's overarching life purpose, it is nearly impossible to be a true revolutionary leader.

If you're not improving upon or adding to what's been done, then you're not really part of a revolution, and you're definitely not being a leader. So many people go through their whole life being busy, busy, busy — but seldom doing much of deep or lasting significance.

Revolutionary leaders do it differently. They focus on what is most significant.

When you know what's been done by the great revolutionary leaders of the past, and you add to the strength and wisdom of their achievements, you will be that much better at doing what still needs to be done in our world today.

You will join the ranks of the reformers, innovators, visionaries, and the right kind of "rascals." If you keep on this path, you'll be a true revolutionary leader. And you can become great.

As Brady and Woodward showed in their best-selling classic book *Launching a Leadership Revolution*, there are many levels of leadership, but the highest level belongs to those "who build leaders, who build leaders, who build leaders." This is revolutionary leadership at its finest.

And this brings us to the crux of the matter: *A very important part of your leadership path is that there are many people out there who will join you in the process of fulfilling your great life purpose — if you make the choice to truly lead. To lead like a revolution is needed.*

These people will become your team, and together you'll achieve a great deal that improves the world. Moreover, the people who could be part of your team are out there. Right now. Waiting.

Waiting for *you*.

Indeed, it is time for you to lead. And to build on the shoulders of great past leaders, including those discussed in the chapters to follow. Let's begin by learning the incredibly important lessons that these five great revolutionary leaders have to teach us.

1723: Runs away from home; arrives in Philadelphia with nothing but two loaves of bread and the dream of a better life.

1724–27: Learns how to be a good printer.

1728: Launches and develops several printing businesses and franchises across the colonies.

1748: Creates the business success to become fully financially free to live his purpose.

1749–75: Writes, invents, founds, creates, and revolutionizes all sorts of fields, from literature and science to media and philanthropy.

1776: Helps draft the Declaration of Independence.

1777–85: Serves as a legendary foreign diplomat.

1787: Helps draft the United States Constitution.

1

BENJAMIN FRANKLIN:

Give Yourself Time to Be Great

Benjamin Franklin is an interesting figure in history, and a powerful revolutionary leader to study, because he fits into both major categories of revolutionary leadership—he was a revolutionary for freedom and against tyranny in a period of societal decline, but he was also a powerful innovator for progress and prosperity during a time of great societal peace and prosperity.

In many ways, Franklin was a visionary, a revolutionary, and a great leader. Likewise, he can be a great mentor to those who wish to achieve success, make a difference, and improve the world today.

One of the most profound lessons he taught, both through example and in words, was the importance of giving yourself time to be great.

This lesson can take a number of forms, and all are vitally important to genuine revolutionary leadership. Those who never give themselves time to be great will simply never achieve their potential, no matter how much they think they want to.

People who know that time matters tend to have more effective and meaningful lives than those who don't realize time matters.

Missing out on success, happiness, greatness, or whatever it is you're working toward, just because you don't give yourself adequate time, would be a serious letdown.

Unfortunately that hasn't stopped many, many people in history from doing just that.

Franklin, however, is a shining example of how to make time for important things, and both his life and his teachings provide helpful insight for those who want to skip mediocrity and wisely give themselves time to be great!

"Do not squander time for that is the stuff life is made of."

It's easy to say we stand for greatness—and even to mean it—but it's much harder to live a truly great life.

Moreover, there are two ways to give ourselves time for greatness. One is simply to be patient, to work hard to build great things, and to keep working at them long enough to bring about the fruits of our labors. The second way to give ourselves time for greatness is equally important: we need to truly use the minutes and hours of our lives doing things that actually bring greatness!

Historically speaking, very few people who ultimately fall short of greatness in life do so because they sat down as kids and decided to aim for mediocrity. And even though there are a number of people who decide that greatness is too much hard work for them, there are still a lot more people who think and say that they *want* to make a difference than there are leaders who really *do* change the world.

In fact, this section could also be called "Time is Important." And despite the fact that people don't always realize it, time really does matter! Franklin wasn't messing around when he said that it's the stuff life is made of.

People who know that time matters tend to have more effective and meaningful lives than those who don't realize time matters.

At this point, let's turn to Franklin's life. The fact that he gave us the quote at the head of this section suggests that he understood the importance of using time wisely, and his actions show that he put his money, feet, and hands where his mouth was.

How It *Could* Have Ended

Throughout his life, Franklin could have spent his time doing all sorts of things, from moping about the difficulty of his circumstances (as a child, he was sent to live with his older brother who beat and abused him till he ran away) to simply not living his purpose. Instead he chose to invest his time into himself and his mission.

As a person who recognized the value of time, Benjamin Franklin not only sought daily to spend what time he had in ways that were meaningful and significant, he also dedicated years of his life, a significant fortune, and many other important sacrifices so that he would have more time later on in life to spend on the things that mattered most.

> **Great leaders often achieve greatness by consistently asking themselves whether their minutes are mattering in the big picture, and how they can make them matter more.**

In fact, top leader Orrin Woodward summed up the life and character of Benjamin Franklin in one sentence, saying: "Franklin spent money to make time, while most of us spend time to make money."

This is something that most people miss in modern times. Even to most who are great leaders today, the idea of spending money to make *time* was often completely foreign to them when they first

> **"Franklin spent money to make time, while most of us spend time to make money."**

started their leadership journey. This is simply not a value in most places today.

For many people, in short, time seems like the lesser value, existing as a resource mainly to be spent making money. And in turn, money is too valuable to be spent on real time, meaningful life experiences, and other such things. Instead, many people seek to save their precious money for things that "matter," such as paying bills, buying food or even toys, and affording bigger loans and more debt.

While we agree that it is important to pay bills, get out of debt, and even enjoy yourself, we also recognize that the mind-set that leaves individuals rushing to spend their time making money leaves little time for greatness in the end.

> **If you want your life to be about something, you have to find a way to make your time about that thing. Until you do, your life is about something else. Period.**

Again, this idea is completely foreign to most people today. Yet Franklin understood it deeply and lived a hugely significant life because of it.

Revolutionary and visionary leaders who hope to give themselves time to be great should start by learning from Franklin to value time—and use money to fund more of it—as the substance of life. In reality, money can be important as

> **Revolutionary leaders who hope to give themselves time to be great should start by learning from Franklin to value time—instead of money—as the substance of life.**

a powerful tool to increase one's effectiveness at wisely using and investing time, but it shouldn't be confused for the actual substance of life.

Make It Count by *Counting* It!

Those who don't understand how much time matters or who fail to see that life is made up of a bunch of smaller pieces of time, often fail to achieve greatness simply because they try to live a great life without living a bunch of great decades, years, weeks, hours, or minutes.

Life is made up of time, which means it is made up of hours and minutes. Great leaders often achieve greatness by consistently asking themselves whether their hours and minutes are mattering in the big picture, and how they can make them matter more.

For example, it's clear that hours and minutes mattered deeply to Franklin, because he found that in hours and minutes he could do an awful lot.

Without hours and minutes, how do you discover the connection between lightning and electricity? Or found a library? Or negotiate a treaty that's pivotal in the history of freedom? Or do anything that matters?

Granted, in our day hours and minutes can also be spent watching television, playing video games, exploring YouTube threads, or getting involved in the endless drama of politically charged Facebook rants. And while there may be a place and time for such pursuits, understanding the power and value of hours and minutes — and choosing to invest them in the right things, places, and ways—are crucial to revolutionary leadership.

Perhaps the main reason that so many people who would rather be "great than not" end up with the "not" instead of the great, is that they don't understand that life is made up of time. They mean to spend their *lives* doing good or being great, but they spend their *time* doing something else. This is a very big deal.

It comes down to this: if you want your life to be about something, you have to find a way to make your time about that thing. Until you do, your life is about something else. Period.

How you spend your time, how you spend your hours and minutes, really is how you spend your life. Leaders understand this, and so instead of squandering their time, they make their minutes, hours, and lives about their purpose.

"There will be sleeping enough in the grave."

Of course, it's not enough to simply value time (although that's a pretty good start, and if everyone in the world began applying this one rule, the whole world would improve drastically); you also have to start using it!

We hear frequently that the most successful man in the world has the same number of hours in the day as the least successful, and everyone in between is on the same clock.

Yet there is a significant difference in what they each accomplish.

The combination of realizing that time matters, and using the time you have with the mindset that sleeping is for the next life, works wonders on what one can accomplish.

Obviously Franklin didn't mean to say that leaders and successful people should never sleep till they're dead. If he had, he'd have been dead a lot sooner. In fact, another popular quote from his writings, which he truly lived by, says, "Early to bed and early to rise makes a man healthy, wealthy, and wise."

Nevertheless, he and many others who have achieved great success did so by living intentionally and effectively utilizing the time they were given.

LIVE BY THIS VERY IMPORTANT →

Time is a nonrefundable and limited resource that is endowed to us for the purpose of "doing greatness." In this sense, "give yourself time to be great" could simply mean that you *accept* the time you've been given to be great and use it in a way that truly fulfills your stewardship and responsibility

> **Using the time you have with the mindset that sleeping is for the next life works wonders on what one can accomplish.**

as someone who has been given a priceless gift.

What Will You Do with Yours?

Leaders who understand the importance of time and the purpose of time—and remember that time is not a limitless commodity — use their hours and minutes differently. This is often the difference between a successful 24 hours and a less successful day.

In the life of Benjamin Franklin we can see a series of highly successful 24-hour periods strung together to make a revolutionary life. A revolutionary life consists of steadily revolutionary hours and minutes, day after day.

> **Time matters. Especially when you *make* it matter.**

Of course, a truly successful revolutionary minute isn't always what we'd imagine to be that of a successful leader. In his early days, Franklin was certainly less than successful, if you take his minutes one at a time.

As a young man he had "friends" cross to the other side of the street when they saw him coming, in order to avoid interaction with him. This at a time when crossing the street wasn't exactly a picnic. Unpaved streets of the era (which Franklin later helped improve) were often either dusty or muddy, not to mention the normal difficulties caused by the chaotic traffic of passing carriages and riders.

However, all this was worth the hassle to his peers, if it meant avoiding Franklin. To put it simply, he was known as over-opinionated, inconsiderate, and even downright rude!

Yet even at this time in his life, Franklin's minutes could be categorized as highly successful revolutionary minutes, because

> **A revolutionary life consists of steadily revolutionary hours and minutes, day after day.**

he chose to live them intentionally, which meant that over time each minute saw him getting better as a leader and as a person.

He actually *chose* how to spend his time, every minute of it, so each minute strung *together* to make a gradually improving *him*. Each minute led to even *better* minutes.

At some point, he had a friend—perhaps "associate" would be more accurate—who was bold enough to inform him that everyone hated him! That he was terrible to be around.

For many, this would have been a time to get defensive, to turn against the messenger, and to continue on as a difficult person. But Franklin didn't get caught up in the egotistical opportunities presented to him by this conversation, instead deciding to use his time wisely for self-improvement.

Upon hearing this unpleasant remark from his associate, he truly took it to heart and decided that if he wanted to matter, to be a real leader, he'd need to learn how to deal with, love, serve, and appreciate people. This is where his famous thirteen virtues came from.

He spent grueling hours and minutes giving himself time to be great, as he made mistakes, as he failed, and as he practiced being a better friend instead of always being "right."

To some, it might seem unemotional, robotic, or even deviously manipulative to *practice* being a friend, yet Franklin understood that to be truly great, he had to *learn* to love and serve the people around him in meaningful and helpful ways.

And so he invested the time it took to do just that.

Benjamin Franklin's 13 Virtues

Here are some of the daily rules for himself that Franklin came up with to overcome these challenges:

2-Silence. Speak not but what may benefit others or yourself; avoid trifling conversation.

3-Order. Let all your things have their places; let each part of your business have its time.

4-Resolution. Resolve to perform what you ought; perform without fail what you resolve.

5-Frugality. Make no expense but to do good to others or yourself; i.e., waste nothing.

6-Industry. Lose no time; be always employ'd in something useful; cut off all unnecessary actions.

11-Tranquillity. Be not disturbed at trifles, or at accidents common or unavoidable.

13-Humility. Imitate Jesus and Socrates.

Just consider how much time and effort it took to figure out, polish, and then fully live such virtues! But because Franklin gave himself this time, and truly used it, he became known, and is still known today, as one of history's most effective people and one of the world's greatest diplomats. That's a major shift: from a real "jerk" to a world-class diplomat.

Time matters. Especially when you *make* it matter.

This is one of the most significant ways to apply the principle of giving yourself time to be great. Of course, there are a few other deep (and deeply *effective*) nuances to consider in order to make this lesson really pop, and luckily, Franklin didn't stop there*!*

"Don't confuse motion with action."

Another important detail to keep in mind when it comes to how you spend your time is the fact that busyness and effectiveness are not always the same thing. (In fact, bus-i-ness and effectiveness are not always the same thing either.)

Using your daily 1,440 minutes effectively doesn't mean simply using them, or even just using them on something besides sleep, laziness, or frivolity.

In order to be truly effective, productive, and genuinely great, leaders must go a step beyond using lots of the minutes at their disposal, and learn to be using those minutes *wisely*. This means not just using them well, but using them in the *best*, and truly *right* way.

Many people, even some of those who seek to be top leaders and highly effective and successful individuals, spend most of their time feeling extremely busy, but without accomplishing much that truly matters. This is sad on at least two counts, because always feeling drained and exhausted isn't much *fun*, and accomplishing only meaningless things isn't much *good*.

Unfortunately, while the negative aspects of this type of time management tend to be fairly obvious when articulated, few people who are caught in such a rut even realize they have this problem. Even fewer know what to do about it when they do realize their situation.

Thankfully, since this problem has been around for a while, we can learn from others who have achieved huge success in life by overcoming this very challenge. Franklin himself, aside from having a great deal to *say* on the subject, is an excellent example of how to overcome menial busyness and achieve real, effective results in whatever field matters to you.

Work Smart...

It would have been easy for Franklin to work for forty-plus years at a newspaper, doing much the same things each day, working practically the same hours, and having very little to show for it at the end aside from the regular and fair salary that bought his food, clothes, and housing along the way.

> **Always feeling drained and exhausted isn't much *fun*, and accomplishing only meaningless things isn't much *good*.**

In this alternative version of history: he worked very hard year after year. He stayed quite busy along the way but was still able to find moments of enjoyment here and there.

He worked until he couldn't any more and then lived as simply as he could in order to prolong his existence as much as possible at the end. He led a simple life and was generally happy. He was a good printer's assistant. But while he was always doing *something*, he rarely did anything *great*.

He is not remembered in the history books, and no one knows his name.

But this alternative tale is not his story.

Instead, he spent the first forty years of his life, not only *busy*, but choosing to be extremely *effective*.

He worked not only *hard*, but *smart*. He did not own *many* things, but the *right* things.

And because he lived the first half of his life in this way, he was able to spend his next forty years changing the world and providing truly great service and leadership.

This is another important way that Benjamin Franklin shows us how to give ourselves time to be great. Simply put:

Do the things now that will allow you to do truly great things later.

Simple words. True, powerful, and revolutionary words.

But Still Work *Hard*!

The process Franklin went through is extremely important. Doing the right things and working smart doesn't mean you shouldn't work hard.

Quite the opposite: It's important to be extremely busy doing the right things that will truly bring success.

Benjamin Franklin worked incredibly hard those first forty years. When he was only 16 years old, after a less than ideal childhood, Franklin left his home and went out into the world, traveling from Boston and ultimately ending up in Philadelphia. He knew no one, he had nowhere to go, and after purchasing a couple of rolls, he had nothing.

At this point, as Woodward said, "He had nothing but the drive to improve himself on a daily basis."

Indeed, it's fair to say he was starting at ground zero, having left everything he had and knew to go to a new city, with the hope of creating a new life for himself.

He had a dream, and nothing to go with it but his wholly inadequate self. But he was determined to become something and someone.

So he apprenticed himself out to a printer, and that began his journey.

Start Now

Even early on, Franklin understood the importance of saving money, and he focused on living below his means. During this early period of his life, he decided that instead of spending money on the kinds of meals his peers enjoyed, he'd become a vegetarian who skipped lunch, so he'd be able to save more and spend more on books.

With this attitude, he spent the next few years learning everything he could from his apprenticeship and his reading, until he became a better printer than the man he worked for. When he reached this point, he decided it was time for him to go into business for himself.

Although many didn't believe he could do it, and even his father refused to invest in him, Franklin was determined to earn success, and he was willing to work and sacrifice to get there.

Thankfully, he had already created the important leadership habits of spending less than he made, reading a lot, investing in his own mind, and saving, saving, saving. And when the pressure was on, he started saving, reading, learning and working even more!

After a lot of extra work and sacrifice, he was able to save enough to start his own printing shop. Of course, he wasn't exactly in the clear yet, and he was working way more than was comfortable.

But he kept living the lifestyle he'd learned in his youth: learn, work, save. And a few years later he received and *recognized* the opportunity that led to the freedom he'd need to become the great man we know about today.

Make It Who You Are

Because of the excellence he achieved in his trade, he was sought after to start print shops in several other cities, and because he had saved up so much capital throughout his life and had invested in his mind by wide reading, he was able to partner with eight different people to set up print shops all over the colonies—partnerships that gave him partial ownership of (and a third of the profit from) eight of the 17 major American newspapers of the time.

By sacrificing and working so much at the beginning, and in all the right ways, he was able to set himself up for the rest of his life. Again, since he worked hard, lived below his means, saved a lot, and truly invested in himself along the way, he was able to live a lifestyle that would have seemed impossible to anyone who saw him walking down the street at age 16, in wet, dirty clothes, eating a loaf of bread, and without a friend or penny to his name.

> **Franklin spent the early years of his life consistently doing the right things, so that when the call to greatness came, he truly had time to answer it.**

Not only did he end up making a few friends and pennies, but because of the way he lived, by the end of his life he had enough money coming in from the residual income stream he had created for himself that he could have lived hundreds and hundreds of years longer, whether he ever worked again or not. And he had a large congregation of friends who dearly loved him.

But still, he went a step further.

"Well done is better than well said."

Franklin spent the early years of his life consistently doing the right things, so that when the call to greatness came, he truly had time to answer it.

As a young man, he set out to achieve the kind of success that meant he'd never have to work another day in his life, and by the time he was 42 years old, he had obtained it. But that wasn't enough.

For the rest of his life, while he certainly took time for leisure and even pleasure, he worked hard, sacrificed greatly, and lived below his means, but instead of doing it to make a living, he did much of it to leave a legacy.

He spent the next 40 years of his life working hard, not because he had to, but because he knew he was *meant* to. He knew he was meant for something greater, a greater purpose, and he dedicated his life to it.

And because he did this, he was able to do all kinds of important things in his life.

Getting Stuff Done

To begin with, the successes and victories included in the process of Franklin's own personal journey to the top were not devoid of meaning and significance in the lives of others. Because he was the man he was, even his own triumphs meant triumph for the world. Just consider:

- Benjamin Franklin set up the world's first franchise model.
- He created a number of inventions, including the Franklin stove and the first bifocal lens.

- He founded several important institutions and community service organizations such as libraries, fire departments, and a university.
- He contributed in important ways to almost every significant American founding document of freedom.
- He served as American's ambassador and delegate and directly protected and increased his nation's freedom and prosperity.
- His writings spread far and wide and taught principles of leadership and wisdom to readers throughout the colonies and in Europe.

In reference to Franklin, Woodward went on to say, "You can't spend money to buy time, unless you're willing to sacrifice the short term for the long term."

This is exactly what Benjamin Franklin did, and it revolutionized the world! In art, science, business, leadership, freedom, and countless other areas, Benjamin Franklin was a revolutionary leader, and because of him, the world will never be the same.

"Never leave that till tomorrow which you can do today."

There are many different ways that revolutionaries must interpret and apply the words "give yourself time to be great," and we can only really dig into a few here. Likewise, there are many different lessons we could learn from Benjamin Franklin's life, and only a few are included here.

In fact, because he had so much time in the last half of his life to dedicate to nothing other than greatness, we could pick out quotes and lessons from him on almost any topic and they'd be among the best available in the world.

In many ways he truly gave himself time for greatness! He gave himself time, and then he took that time and worked to *be* great.

This is what made him a revolutionary leader.

> **In art, science, business, leadership, freedom, and countless other areas, Benjamin Franklin was a revolutionary leader, and because of him, the world will never be the same.**

Franklin started young and achieved complete free time for greatness by his early forties. But even if you missed that age, it's not too late for you to find, make, or *give* yourself the time it will take to be a great revolutionary leader.

By applying the lessons taught through Benjamin Franklin's example, and beginning your journey today—this *hour*, this *minute*—you can become a great revolutionary leader.

Franklin accomplished what he did because he started spending his minutes and hours on greatness, which led to a life of greatness. You can do the same.

Today. Give yourself time to be great by carving out minutes in your already busy life to invest in greatness.

Give yourself time to be great by dedicating the time you already have to greatness by connecting your minutes in a way that will lead to a better you.

Give yourself time to be great by living the next month and year of your life in a way that will leave you more free to answer when the call to be great comes to you.

Give yourself time to be great by recognizing that it really will *take* time. It's not going to happen all at once, so be patient with yourself, and just keep improving every minute, every day, every week. Choose wisely how to spend each hour.

Take control of your hours. Devote them to the right activities, the pursuits that will bring greatness.

Be patient, but do the right deeds that will *make* you great by the end. Franklin said: "If a man empties his purse into his head, no man can take it from him. An investment in knowledge pays the best interest." And he used some of his money to buy books—and then he read them. You can do the same thing! Use your time to *become* great.

Time is what life is made of, so live a great life by choosing to be great for at least a few hours a day.

As leaders today strive to learn from Franklin's example and his words, they must take life by the horns and truly *give* themselves time for greatness. For those who do this, greatness will be within reach.

A revolution of greatness is needed, but you have to give yourself time. Starting now. This hour. This minute.

1760: Passes examination in Williamsburg, Virginia, and becomes a lawyer.

1765: Elected to the House of Burgesses and presents his 7 Resolutions against the Stamp Act and the Caesar-Brutus speech.

1775: Delivers famous "Give me Liberty, or Give me Death!" speech.

1776–86: Serves as Virginia's military commander, Governor, and member of the House of Delegates.

1787: Rejects appointment to represent Virginia at the Constitutional Convention, in order to stand for local rule.

1788: Powerfully opposes the proposed constitution at the Virginia Ratification Convention, ultimately influencing the drafting and passing of the Bill of Rights.

1799: Delivers his final speech at Charlotte Courthouse, and dies later the same year.

2

PATRICK HENRY

Surround Yourself with Greatness

atrick Henry is well known for being more than a little bit revolutionary. Even his friends, colleagues, and contemporaries viewed him as direct, bold, and uncompromising.

They knew precisely what he stood for, because he made it very clear. And they knew that he would stand for it to his last breath.

Being a man of character so strong that it *becomes* reputation is a powerful thing, and this is exactly the type of man Patrick Henry was. He is remembered most as the man who stood and uttered the famous lines, "Give me liberty, or give me death," in the face of the greatest world power in his day, because he believed in something important.

Moreover, he spurred his nation to take on a world power and then actually beat them.

Granted, he wasn't even close to standing alone against King George III, Parliament, or the British army and navy, yet he was the type of man who would probably have spoken just as loudly, and every bit as firmly, had he been standing all by himself and less than a yard away from the entire force of Great Britain's might.

Henry was unquestionably a man of great courage and greatness, and the fact that he was willing to fight against such a huge world power at the time, having only a few farmers, merchants, and colonial lawyers and preachers on his side, speaks volumes about his conviction, his courage, and his willingness to demand greatness of himself and of the world around him.

> **Being a man of character so strong that it *becomes* reputation is a powerful thing.**

In fact, the reality that he *wasn't* all by himself actually adds to his importance as a revolutionary leader, because it shows he was actually *leading*, and it also makes the list of lessons we can learn from him a lot longer.

Patrick Henry was a man who boldly said what needed to be said, even when doing so meant a lot of trouble for him. And, because he was also a man who boldly *lived* the meaningful words he spoke, his life and words combine to teach us a number of invaluable lessons about revolutionary leadership.

> ## *"The battle, sir, is not to the strong alone; it is to the vigilant, the active, the brave."*

Early in his life, Henry decided he was going to become a lawyer. At that time in history, you didn't necessarily go to school to become an attorney. Sometimes you would read and study on your own, or you'd study under the mentoring of a lawyer or spend money to be trained by one.

Patrick Henry didn't really have a lot of money, and he couldn't afford to do much preparation at all. But he decided that he was going to be a lawyer, and he set out to do his best to make it happen. After doing a bit of reading, he decided he was ready to achieve his dream.

Under the rules of the time, the requirements to become a lawyer were basically that you had to be interviewed by three qualified lawyers, and if they thought you had studied enough, really understood the law well enough, and were actually qualified and ready, they'd sign off and say that you were ready to practice law.

> **Patrick Henry was a man who boldly said what needed to be said, even when doing so meant a lot of trouble for him.**

Go Bold

When Patrick Henry went to be interviewed by his three lawyers, the first person he met with was George Wythe, who was known as the mentor to many of the most influential and best-known American founders, including Thomas Jefferson and James Madison, among others. Wythe was considered one of the top lawyers and judges of the day. And there was Patrick Henry, after only a little bit of studying, ready to interview with the best lawyer in colonial America.

Thirty minutes into the interview George Wythe stopped the discussion and informed young Patrick Henry that he wouldn't even consider signing off because Henry understood nothing of the law.

Nevertheless, Patrick Henry still wanted to be a lawyer. And although continuing on his quest might have seemed crazy to some, since he was so clearly not the obvious or accepted version of a deeply-studied lawyer, Henry did continue.

He was willing to learn to be great even if it seemed like he wasn't naturally talented at it.

The fact that Henry chose the best lawyer in the colony as his first meeting shows a willingness to be vigilant, active, and brave, even if he wasn't precisely "well read." Patrick Henry knew that he wasn't perfect and didn't have the advantages of money and long-tutored learning, but he also knew that he had something important to share with the world, and he wanted to be a lawyer.

Perseverance pays off

Don't Go Home!

So he went on to test himself, to push himself to the limits and to learn more and improve. He had started the process, and then he just kept pushing. Henry went to those who had the results he was looking for, those he wanted to be like, and he kept doing the

> **Surrounding yourself with greatness is a vital piece of true and effective revolutionary leadership.**

hard work of becoming great and surrounding himself with greatness.

Patrick Henry knew that in order to win the game, he'd need to be one of the players. He chose to understand greatness, do what he could to achieve it, and surround himself with it in every way he could.

Of course, the story doesn't end there.

Even after facing the reality of his uphill battle and receiving this initial rejection and failure, Patrick Henry was determined to achieve his dreams, and he refused to let anything stop him.

While he remembered this experience and let it shape him (so much that he followed Wythe's mentoring and ultimately became better acquainted with the law), he also knew that to surround himself with greatness he had to choose to make his surroundings great.

By continuing his personal battle to become a lawyer, and also upgrading his education by reading the books recommended to him by mentors, he was self-selecting for greatness. This is an important lesson for prospective leaders to learn, both as it applies to themselves and to those they interact with along their journey.

Henry's quote that heads this section is powerful! One of the ways to be great, and to be surrounded with and by greatness, is to _choose_ to be great and to team up with others who choose the same.

> **Leaders are the ones who forget the odds and the statistics that say they'll never amount to much and simply lead anyway.**

So he kept at it! He didn't quit or give up; instead, he went and found someone else to help him reach his dreams. He continued his search and went on to get interviewed by other lawyers.

The next lawyer he met with was a bit more gracious but likewise stopped the interview after about half an hour and told him he that whatever other gifts and talents he had, he simply didn't know the law. However, this man, after making him promise to study up on a specific list of books, agreed to sign off on his qualification.

Even though Henry wasn't a great lawyer—as two of his mentors were quick to tell him—he made the _choice_ to be great, which meant all that was left was the work.

> **Oftentimes the best leaders aren't necessarily the ones who seemed best cut out for it to begin with, but the ones who self-select.**

In this way, he wasn't exactly "prepared," but he was absolutely "vigilant, active, and brave"! Leaders understand that vigilance, action, and courage are some of the most important characteristics of those who truly change themselves and the world — so they develop these qualities of greatness and revolutionary leadership. And as mentioned above, they surround themselves with people who are also focusing on such skills.

Patrick Henry's life and words are a fantastic example of the fact that everyone is invited to the battle! And great leaders and visionaries can come from anywhere.

Self-Selection

Oftentimes the best leaders aren't necessarily the ones who seemed best cut out for it to begin with, but the ones who self-select — the ones who forget the odds and the statistics that say they'll never amount to much and simply lead anyway. Patrick Henry was just such a leader, and he surrounded himself with other

> **It isn't just the strong or the naturally gifted who are needed in the battle and who can make a difference.**

such revolutionaries, which contributed greatly to his success in life and ultimately led to his greatest victories.

At this point, having one of the three signatures he needed and keeping a "can-do" mind-set, Patrick Henry kept going.

Next he came to the Randolph brothers. Both were lawyers, and they agreed to interview him.

The first brother very quickly realized that Patrick Henry didn't know the law. But he continued the interview, and when he came to the topic of natural law, something shifted. Not only did Patrick Henry understand a bit of natural law, he was actually able to hold his own and debate it with John Randolph, who was interviewing him!

John Randolph realized throughout the interview that even though Patrick Henry had never read the many law books that most lawyers had, he understood natural law — the idea of great moral laws of God and the universe — on a level that was beyond even his own.

In response to being bested on the topic of natural law by someone who clearly hadn't studied or read as much as he had about it, Randolph said, "From this lesson you have given me... I will never trust your appearance again."

NEVER JUDGE A BOOK BY ITS COVER

Tenacity Wins

Eventually Henry got his dream and became a barrister in colonial America, but perhaps the important lesson to learn from all this is that sometimes the greatest people with the greatest talents or the greatest potential aren't always easily recognizeable.

> By learning truth, leaders are able to start doing an incredible thing— they are able to begin actually using and *applying* truth in their own lives.

They aren't always the ones who *seem* ready for greatness, but rather the ones who are willing to surround themselves with greatness and take the steps to get themselves there too. When it comes to surrounding yourself with greatness, remember that everyone is invited! It's not just the obvious or seemingly "natural" leaders who are needed and who are *great*. The battle is for the vigilant, the active, and the brave as well! Just ask Patrick Henry.

"For my part, whatever anguish of spirit it may cost, I am willing to know the whole truth; to know the worst and to provide for it."

Another of the most important principles to discuss in a study of Patrick Henry and how to surround yourself with greatness, is the importance of simply seeking truth — hard truth, ugly truth, happy truth, and glorious truth.

By learning truth, leaders are able to start doing an incredible thing — they are able to begin actually using and *applying* truth in their own lives. This is key to leadership.

While it may be hard to accept certain truths, and while finding out about difficult realities might make reality in general seem a lot tougher, it is much better to have the opportunity to overcome, counteract, or provide for such truths than to simply remain victims or slaves to them out of sheer ignorance. * LEARN THIS BECAUSE MOST DON'T

Ignorance, Termites, and Gratitude

Consider, for example, the story told by Orrin Woodward of a man who happens to notice what he thinks might be a termite crawling under the side of his house as he comes home from work one day.

As he goes to investigate, he learns that he was not only correct in his original assumption that the creature was a termite but that his whole house and all his walls are quite full of them and in danger of complete collapse at any moment!

> **Rather than being bliss, ignorance is more often simply slavery and bondage.**

VERY GOOD

Now, this problem seems completely insurmountable. On his budget, the chance of finding and actually affording the right equipment to remove the problem without totally destroying his whole house appears quite slim.

On the other hand, leaving it and risking not only his house but his own life if the walls decide to come down on their own doesn't seem like a very good idea either. And the possibility of simply moving seems all but impossible.

In frustration and regret at his circumstances, the man finds himself wishing he'd never happened upon the termite—despite the fact that seeing the little guy has in all likelihood saved his life.

Now, in life, hard truths don't always come in such an obviously helpful way as they do in this story. In all honesty, while the man could find himself regretting the situation he finds himself in, he does have a hard time *really* wishing he'd never learned about the harsh reality.

Simply put, before he knew about the problem, he was powerless to fix it.

Face It!

Patrick Henry understood that rather than being bliss, ignorance is more often simply slavery and bondage. At every chance, he chose to face reality—even when it wasn't pleasant—and make the most of it with the power and capacity he had to *make* his life his own. This is a vital part of leadership.

While some truths certainly hurt, he understood that by knowing them, he could actually *do* something about them! Something he'd never be able to accomplish if he didn't know about them in the first place.

For example, when the Stamp Act was hitting the American colonies full force, even though many were tempted to skirt the issue, downplay the importance of what was happening, or ignore the facts, Patrick Henry knew that the truth mattered. He

> **We are still living off the ripple effects of his courage in that moment and throughout his life.**

knew that in order to have and preserve freedom, leaders and people in positions of influence and power would need to stand up for the truth. And so he did just that.

He decided to take a stand and not only *learn* the truth but fight for it boldly, even when it hurt. Because he felt so strongly and stood so uncompromisingly for the truth in this situation, his character demanded that other leaders do the same, and the impact on freedom was incredible.

We are still benefitting from the ripple effects of his courage in that moment and throughout his life.

At that point he was a part of the legislature of Virginia, and while the rest of the group was in the process of drafting an appeasing response to the offenses and cruelties involved with the Stamp Act, Patrick Henry was preparing to present one of the boldest lists of resolutions the British Empire had ever seen, calling out the government for wrongdoing and asserting the rights of the people. It was a turning point in world history.

Go Big!

His boldness was a beacon of light for those around him, and it demanded courage and action of all who came into contact with it.

Although not all of his proposed resolutions were passed by the Virginia House of Burgesses, the way they were recorded and published made others assume they had been fully adopted, giving other colonies the courage to be likewise daring, and this led in large part to the bold stance the colonies took in the revolution itself.

This brashness was part of what allowed for the height of success the Americans experienced and achieved in the form of actual independence and real freedom—much more than most revolutions of its kind have even dreamed of throughout history.

All this because one man refused to hide from or even soften the truth. Instead, he chose to face it. In doing this, he was surrounding himself with the greatness of truth itself, and it inspired many others to take the same bold step toward greatness as well, thus bringing countless others to the cause.

By standing for truth, Henry chose greatness in a huge and meaningful way that gave him greater opportunity to fulfill his life purpose and change the world as a revolutionary leader.

This is powerful, and it leads directly to the next important lesson from Patrick Henry.

KNOW THIS

"The eternal difference between right and wrong does not fluctuate, it is immutable."

Patrick Henry also surrounded himself with greatness by simply recognizing that he was already surrounded by greatness, no matter what he did or whose side he chose to be on!

Specifically, he recognized that right and wrong exist regardless of his views, allegiance, understanding, etc. He realized that right and wrong are not only independent of him, but immutable! And recognizing this, he chose to ally himself with right and so with greatness.

He understood, as all true and effective leaders must, that there is a true right and a real

> **He understood, as all true and effective leaders must, that there is a true right and a real wrong.**

wrong; there is, ultimately, really no neutral. He knew this and then he acted accordingly.

When the difficulties and oppressions that led to the Revolutionary War came, Patrick Henry could have found many different easy ways out, rather than standing for what he knew was right.

He could have sought out special deals for himself, his family, or his colony. He could have justified this by saying that his constituents needed this very thing from him.

He could even have saved himself a lot of trouble by simply speaking out a little less often, or a little less loudly, or simply a little *less*. Yet he knew that each of these options would have been a failure to stand for right, which would have been the same as serving wrong.

> **When it comes to being a revolutionary leader, one of the most important things you need is other people.**

And so, at every chance, Patrick Henry chose to stand, call for the floor, and speak boldly.

He was courageous, visionary, and revolutionary. He surrounded himself with greatness by recognizing it where it was and standing for it at every turn.

All In!

He became a great leader, and ultimately changed the world, because he learned to recognize greatness and allied himself with it fully and completely.

As the revolution in America continued to heat up, to the point that Massachusetts was at war with Britain, the legislative body of Virginia—of which Henry was still a part—met to decide what they should do, how they should act, and which side they should stand by in the conflict. In this intense situation, Henry received, and accepted, another powerful call to great revolutionary leadership.

At the time, they had to meet in a different town than usual, because the danger of arrest or punishment was so great in their normal meeting place. Many in the group sought to remain neutral or even somehow realign themselves with Britain, rather than coming to the aid of their neighbors who were under occupation up in Boston and risking the full force of Britain's wrath.

But Patrick Henry knew that something else was needed, so he stood for what he knew was right!

After arguing for the importance of standing up for freedom for a good long while, Patrick Henry stood and threw himself entirely on the side of right by delivering the famous "Give me liberty, or give me death" speech, holding nothing back. By sheer force of his own dedication to what mattered, his example and leadership demanded that others put aside their excuses and stand also.

After boldly teaching the legislature a number of important principles and inspiring the audience of his peers in his powerful way, Henry closed by saying:

"It is vain, sir, to extenuate the matter.
Gentlemen may cry, peace, peace, but there is no peace.
The war is actually begun!
The next gale that sweeps from the north will bring
to our ears the clash of resounding arms!

Our brethren are already in the field!
Why stand we idly here?
What is it that gentlemen wish?
What would they have?
Is life so dear, or peace so sweet, as to be
purchased at the price of chains and slavery?
Forbid it, Almighty God!
I know not what course others may take;
but as for me,
give me liberty or give me death!"

These are only a few of the powerful words he uttered in this speech, yet they speak volumes about the kind of man and the kind of leader he was. In fact, the years of reading and leadership had turned Patrick into a man who was now a far cry from that boy who had tried to get his first two legal mentors to sign off on his readiness to practice law. He was now able to get nearly a whole continent to sign up for war!

The Power of What's Right

To be a truly great revolutionary leader, one must know right from wrong and then place himself so firmly and boldly in the camp of that immutable and unfluctuating right, that there can never be confusion as to whose side he is on. This is part of what it means to truly *lead*.

Revolutionary leaders, like Patrick Henry, lead out greatly. In part, they lead by being so bold about which side they're on (and being on the right side) that others naturally follow their passion, strength, and courage.

Interestingly, just as the small quote above was only a tiny part of the speech it came from, the speech itself was a mere fraction of the boldness and leadership that marked the life of Patrick Henry.

He was a man who knew right and stood for it even if he had to stand alone. However, he took his leadership beyond this level in a powerful way and helped many others choose the path of right.

"United we stand, divided we fall."

Indeed, when it comes to being a revolutionary leader, one of the most important things you need is other people. Being a leader at all means that you have other people following you, or if not, as John Maxwell reminds us, "You're just out for a walk."

And while a revolution of one might still be powerful, it's not really a revolution at all without allies, teammates, and real community. Rather, it's just a demonstration.

We said earlier in the chapter that Patrick Henry was the type of leader who would have stood against Britain all by himself if necessary, and from everything he said and did in his life, we think this is true. Yet the fact that he didn't settle for a revolution of one — but brought many others into the cause—is a powerful example to leaders today who would change and improve the world.

Leaders *Lead*

Patrick Henry was a true visionary and revolutionary, and as such he was a truly great man. But by surrounding himself with greatness on all sides, demanding and *inspiring* greatness in others and leading the charge, he was not *only* a great speaker, a great rebel, or even a great man, but a truly great revolutionary *leader*.

This is so important!

It matters that those who were born for greatness stand up and choose it. But on top of this, it is deeply crucial that such individuals go a step further and bring others with them—*leading* others to revolutionary leadership!

> It's a great and powerful thing to be the kind of person who will stand up for what's right, no matter what others are doing, but it's even greater to bring an army of revolutionary leaders with you when you do it!

Following this example will make the work you do more effective, and often easier. But more important than that, it will make your greatness matter on a much higher level!

By surrounding himself with greatness, Patrick Henry deeply changed the world in major ways. He helped others to take the plunge and to be great also.

He was one of the most pivotal leaders of the American Revolution and ultimately

of American freedom, because he self-selected himself
for greatness and then led others to do the same, and the
change he made in doing so is still alive over two hundred
years later.

Patrick Henry invited everyone to join the battle,
whether they seemed like the
perfect candidate or not. He
allowed the vigilant and brave
to take their place beside the
naturally strong in a way that
brought higher levels of
synergy and success than
would have been possible otherwise.

> **Revolutionary leaders surround themselves with greatness, and in doing so, they change the world.**

He was willing to learn the truth — the good, the bad,
and the ugly — and he was bold enough to stand for right,
even when it was hard or nearly impossible.

He surrounded himself with greatness by expecting,
inspiring, and leading others to be great right alongside
him, and because of this, he achieved greatness for himself
and left the opportunity to do the same for countless others
over the next few centuries.

Learning and applying these lessons from Patrick Henry
will make a huge difference in the ability of prospective
leaders to achieve and inspire greatness in our time. Put
simply, revolutionary leaders surround themselves with
greatness, and in doing so, they change the world.

1780: Signed up to help in the Revolutionary War effort as a courier. He was only thirteen years old. In 1781, he was captured by the British. One officer commanded Jackson to clean his boots, and when the fourteen-year-old refused, he was beaten and received a gash on his forehead. He kept the scar for the rest of his life.

1781–96: Educated himself, and with hard work and study, became a lawyer.

1790s: Served in the United States House of Representatives, later the Senate, and then on the Tennessee Supreme Court.

1814–21: Served as a military general and fought battles in the Indian Wars, the War of 1812, and against the Spanish in Florida.

1828–33: As president, he fought an epic battle against the National Bank, including vetoing their renewal charter and withdrawing all government funds.

1835: During his presidency and under his direction and leadership, the United States paid off its entire national debt. It was the only time in history this ever happened.

3

ANDREW JACKSON

Jump into Greatness

When it comes to revolution, leadership, and greatness, Andrew Jackson is a man who simply *must* come up in the conversation.

He was part of the first generation of great Americans, with everything that means. Both in word and in deed, he is a mentor and example to anyone who hopes to change the world by being a revolutionary leader.

From his early life all the way up to his death, Jackson fought a relentless revolution against the status quo. And because he understood and applied important principles, he ended up winning some pretty big victories along the way.

It's powerful to study his battles, his teachings, his victories, and his legacy, because he was a man who unabashedly jumped into greatness and made a difference doing so. Let's dig into what his life has to teach.

"I was born for a storm and a calm does not suit me."

As we've said, Jackson was among the earliest generation of great Americans, and as a teenager he fought in the Revolutionary War. He was scarred when a British soldier sliced his forehead with a knife for refusing to shine the soldier's shoes, and the incident convinced him at a very young age that he hated tyranny.

He hated people forcing others to do things against their will "or suffer the consequences" — and he fought against that idea for the rest of his life. Andrew Jackson also had the courage to stand for what he believed — even when it hurt him personally.

Leaders Must Fight!

He wasn't just a revolutionary in the sense that he shifted thoughts and ideas in a small way — he was a real fighter. He said it himself — he was a man born for a storm! He saw things he wanted to change or protect, and he jumped right in with great courage to fight for them.

From fighting in the Indian Wars in his early days to fighting in the War of 1812, to later getting into politics, and ultimately becoming president of the United States, this was a man who was familiar with fighting. And always, he fought with courage.

> **Leadership also means being able to look at the peaceful calms that would be so much easier than greatness, and having the courage to turn your back on them and take a stand.**

Interestingly, Andrew Jackson's brand of leadership teaches us something truly profound: in a way *all* leadership is revolutionary leadership. If it's not at least a bit revolutionary, it's not really leadership.

Much of Jackson's life, and many of the things he did, involved leading, because he consistently found himself fighting against the mediocrity of the status quo, fighting for freedom, and both embracing and *creating* storms for great revolutionary improvement whenever he saw something that needed to change.

The example of young Andrew refusing to shine the soldier's boot, because he knew it was the right thing to stand against, is merely the beginning. Jackson went far beyond this point throughout his life, but even this tiny moment is a powerful illustration of what it means to be a leader.

To put it bluntly, Andrew Jackson isn't the only person who was born for a storm. In fact, leadership means having the courage to face a storm and ride right into it, *fighting* for the things that matter—even when it means wearing the scars from such storms and battles for the rest of your life.

Leadership also means being able to look at the peaceful calms that would be so much easier than greatness, and having the courage to turn your back on them and take a stand for who you were born to be—a great and *revolutionary* leader.

But of all the battles he fought in his life, if you were to ask him which was his greatest, he would probably answer simply that it was none of his war battles—it was the epic fight he waged against the second U.S. National Bank. In fact, he described the battle thus: "The bank is trying to kill me."

"I try to live my life as if death might come for me at any moment."

But as a man of courage, a leader who stood for what he believed in, and a dedicated fighter, he didn't just sit around waiting for his doom to catch up with him. Instead, he jumped into the battle with his whole heart and his next words were, "But I will kill it."

Orrin Woodward asked the question, "If you knew you couldn't fail, what would you attempt?" This idea is very similar to Jackson's way of living like there's no tomorrow. This perspective usually ends up creating a lifestyle of giving your all to the causes that really matter most.

The proverbial "eat, drink, and be merry, for tomorrow you die," would have looked a lot different if it had been taught by Andrew Jackson. His philosophy was slightly different— actually, pretty much the opposite!

> **Don't wait for greatness to be "thrust upon you" as Shakespeare would say. Rather, *leap* into it and treat it like you have to fight to survive, long before you actually *do*.**

As we see from the quote above, he believed in the idea that we never know when we're going die, so we'd better put our best work in as soon as possible, in case there's not time later.

This led Jackson to a powerful life of seeking out and leading great causes.

The Bank was trying to "kill" him, and he was determined that he'd kill it instead. He hoped he'd have a full lifetime to dedicate to such work, but he wasn't going to depend on that.

Instead, he got down to business right from the start of his presidency—before it, even.

This is part of what it means to jump into greatness— you don't wait for greatness to be "thrust upon you" as Shakespeare would say. Rather, you *leap* into it and treat it like you have to fight to survive, long before you actually *do*.

In his battle with the National Bank, Andrew Jackson did just that.

As Woodward described it: "When he first got involved in the whole thing, some of the big businessmen of the time had teamed up with the government to start this National Bank, and they created it in such a way that they—the banks, the government, and the individuals they wanted to benefit—would have a different set of rules than the ordinary people, making it easier for officials and institutions to get ahead, and harder for the regular people to even keep up.

"Specifically, this involved top-down inflation of the money supply that meant the banks could create money out of thin air virtually any time they—or their cronies—wanted, while everybody else had to pretend the money was real, and act like they were okay with it, all the while watching their own hard-earned pennies mean less and less in the value of the actual market."

Of course, they made it sound a lot better at the time, suggesting that voting for the right people would mean you could get in on the action, claiming that these were superior economic principles that only the experts could understand, that it would boost the economy, and other such deceptive marketing taglines.

Nevertheless, as Woodward put it, they were basically claiming the right—and they were the *only* ones with this right—to print Monopoly money and use it to buy real goods and services. Anyone else trying to print such money would be arrested and prosecuted.

Andrew Jackson, on the other hand, was a populist. He cared about the regular people—about all people—and he knew that when the banks and politicians lived by a different set of rules than the ordinary citizens, it was bad for the economy, and it was bad for freedom.

And so, rather than waiting for the problem to hurt him personally before taking action, he jumped into greatness and fought for right.

Jackson's lesson for us is clear: When it's time to jump into greatness, don't hold back, don't wait, don't get distracted. Jump in!

"Take time to deliberate; but when the time for action arrives, stop thinking and go in."

Jackson was determined to shut down the "Monopoly money."

So he decided to run for president of the United States, promising that if he were elected, he would close the National Bank. Of course, bank experts at the time thought such claims were simply clever campaign tactics and that once he was in office, he'd cave to those who "clearly knew more on the subject than himself." This is the way far too many politicians have acted through history.

> **Those who never do anything rarely lead much other than the do-nothing-brigade— certainly nothing that truly matters.**

Unfortunately for the established power brokers of that time (yet fortunately for the future of freedom and prosperity), they misjudged the measure of the man.

They forgot to consider who he really was and failed to realize that Andrew Jackson was a true revolutionary leader and a man who would leap into greatness at every chance, despite challenges to his personal comforts, preferences, or interests.

He saw a problem, he searched out the solution, he made his plan, and then he simply *did it!*

This is a pivotal aspect of revolutionary leadership.

The saying, "those who can't do, teach" is problematic because the best true teachers are those who show you how it's really done, but history shows that those who never *do* anything rarely lead much other than the do-nothing-brigade—certainly nothing that truly matters.

Talking the Talk

When the powers in Washington and New York assumed that Andrew Jackson was all talk (or all "plan" or all a pie-in-the-sky dreamer), they underestimated the revolutionary leader who would prove to be their biggest opponent in the biggest battle in *their* lives. Because Andrew Jackson meant what he said, and he *did* what he meant.

After campaigning on the promise to defeat the bank and being elected, his first public address as the newly elected president included the following bold and revolutionary statement:

"Both the constitutionality and the expediency of the law creating this bank are well-questioned by a large portion of our fellow citizens, and it must be admitted

by all that it has failed in the great end of establishing a uniform and sound currency."

He recognized that the very reason the bank had been created, the thing it was supposed to fix in the first place, was the thing it was most guilty of perpetrating in society.

> **Andrew Jackson meant what he said, and he *did* what he meant.**

And so, even though he had nearly everything to lose personally from doing so, he chose to act with honor, courage, and conviction, and he jumped into greatness and revolutionary leadership by continuing to do everything in his power to follow through on his promises. He immediately took steps to win the fight.

"Any man worth his salt will stick up for what he believes right...."

This is a powerful statement. It's also very simple. With these words, Andrew Jackson teaches one of the most crucial aspects of revolutionary leadership: find out what's right, stand for it, be bold about it, and never back down. If you're right, be right. And don't be afraid to explain what made you right and invite others to join the team of rightness.

When he vetoed the Second National Bank Charter, he gave a wonderful explanation of what was wrong with it and what he stood for. Here is one of the most powerful sections from his veto message that truly teaches the principles Jackson dedicated his life to promoting:

> *"It is to be regretted that the rich and powerful too often bend the acts of government to their selfish purposes. Distinctions in society will always exist under every just government. Equality of talents, of education, or of wealth cannot be produced by human institutions.*
>
> *"In the full enjoyment of the gifts of Heaven and the fruits of superior industry, economy, and virtue, every man is equally entitled to protection by law; but when the laws undertake to add to these natural and just advantages artificial distinctions, to grant titles, gratuities, and exclusive privileges, to make the rich richer and the potent more powerful, the humble members of society — the farmers, mechanics, and laborers — who have neither the time nor the means of securing like favors to themselves, have a right to complain of the injustice of their government.*
>
> *"There are no necessary evils in government. Its evils exist only in its abuses. If it would confine itself to equal protection, and, as Heaven does its rains, shower its favors alike on the high and the low, the rich and the poor, it would be an unqualified blessing."*

> TRUTH
> **Just as you should be bold about being right, you should also be bold about fixing your mistakes when you've been wrong.**

In modernized laymen's terms what he said was very simple: "If you're doing better than everyone else and it's because you worked hard to get there, good for you—keep living the American Dream! But if you're better off because you took advantage of government power or unjust monopoly to take opportunity from others and live off of their hard work, stop it!

"And if you're the government and you're trying to team up with the richest or most powerful people to make them even richer and more powerful at the expense of everyone else, watch out! I'm shutting you down!"

As Orrin Woodward said, "The American Dream was something we worked for; not something you voted for." Andrew Jackson believed in such ideals, and he also thought it shouldn't be something you paid for with money, titles, "influence," credentials, or anything else other than blood, sweat, tears, and good old-fashioned hard work.

Jump as High as You Can

And so, he jumped into greatness to *keep* it that way, even when many of the richest and most powerful of his time were ferociously opposing both his cause and his efforts.

> **Leaders understand the playing field and they take a stand.**

Of course, none of this should be taken as evidence that you have to be a jerk about things when you're right. In fact, Jackson went on to say that "it takes a slightly better man to acknowledge instantly and without reservation that he is in error." Just as you should be bold about being right, you should also be bold about fixing your mistakes when you've been wrong. As Chris Brady says, "Fight as if you're right, but listen as if you're wrong."

In all this it is key to understand that to be a *leader*, you have to do more than sit in a corner *knowing* what's right but never expressing that knowledge or using it to fix wrongs in meaningful ways. When you're right, you have to be right in the right *ways*, by actually doing something about it.

And you should follow the same pattern when you've been wrong—be *wrong* in the right ways: be wrong *because* you were boldly standing for what you believed in, and rush in with boldness to make things right again when you realize you are in error.

> **There are ultimately no neutrals when it comes to fighting for what's right.**

Jumping into greatness means actually *jumping* in, not just dipping a toe. Don't hold back, give greatness the effort it deserves from you—the effort it *needs*.

"They must be either for, or against us."

One of the reasons it's so important to be bold and truly jump into greatness is the simple truth that there are ultimately no neutrals when it comes to fighting for what's right.

VERY TRUE→

Fence-sitters in the battle for truth, freedom, opportunity, greatness, leadership, etc. are definitely not revolutionary leaders; that much is obvious. Unfortunately, they're also not even revolutionary *followers*.

Sadly, "revolutionary" fence-sitters are actually just guys fighting poorly for the wrong side. As Andrew Jackson taught, if your efforts aren't going toward the right side, it's the same as working for the wrong side.

Leaders understand the playing field and they take a stand. They know the players, the game, the rules, the objective, and the rewards or penalties for winning or losing.

> **"Revolutionary" fence-sitters are actually just guys fighting poorly for the wrong side.**

They know themselves, their friends and their enemies, and they know what they have to do to win. They know what's at stake and who's making what happen.

In Jackson's battle with the bank, enemies were not only clear and evident, they were even declared and aggressively focused on his downfall. Once they realized he was serious in his promise to take them down, the people behind the bank

> **Community is absolutely vital to revolutionary leadership.**

knew they were in trouble, so they started looking for a way to retaliate and ultimately remove Jackson from power so he wouldn't be able to hurt or inconvenience them anymore.

They saw that as president, Jackson was elected by the people and subject to their will for reelection and all future power, so they knew that to get rid of him, they'd need to make the people want to get rid of him.

So they attacked him, not based on what they actually disagreed with, not on policy or principles, but in ways they thought would do the most harm to him with his constituents.

And when Jackson boldly and honestly opposed the unfair and anti-freedom policies and actions of the banks and their supporters by vetoing and openly sharing the dangers of the national bank, his newly made enemies made him the target of all sorts of negativity in the press, seeking to destroy his reputation and any chance he had of getting reelected.

And then they did the unthinkable. In order to hurt him with the people in the way that mattered most, the banks called in all the loans they had given.

Of course, this meant that many businesses and individuals across the United States found themselves in a position of owing a bunch of money they didn't have, and business owners found themselves suddenly losing their businesses.

The goal was to couch this all in such a way that everyone would blame—and therefore hate—Andrew Jackson. However, in doing this, the banks went a little bit too far.

"Without union our independence and liberty would never have been achieved; without union they never can be maintained."

Andrew Jackson knew that a leader has to have a team. In many ways, a leader is only as good as his team. Community is absolutely vital to revolutionary leadership.

With all the attacks and negativity coming at him from his enemies, many people did end up blaming and hating Jackson, but he continued to stand for what he believed in, and as the states watched all of this unfold, many of the state leaders came to realize that the banks really did have too much power over individuals, businesses, the economy, and the nation in general. Many of them started to support Andrew Jackson in his war against the too-powerful banks, and in this way he was able to lead a team against the bank.

Even with the banks trying to centralize and expand their power in a number of ways, Andrew Jackson stood firm. As he did so, others started to realize that what he was doing mattered, and many got on board.

> **Revolutionary leaders by definition do two things: they lead, and they revolutionize.**

When it came time for reelection, Jackson won in a landslide. The people reelected him and stood with him, and he won his battle against the banks so decisively that America had free banking for more than seventy years after his victory. (For where this battle with the banks has taken us today, see Orrin Woodward's *The Financial Matrix*.)

Andrew Jackson was a man who consistently pursued greatness — a man who said what he meant and did what he said, as mentioned, and stood for greatness at every turn.

Because of his firmness and his conviction, he accomplished great things and led a meaningful revolution for freedom and prosperity. This is what it means to be a revolutionary leader. Jump in!

 ## "It's a...poor mind that can think of only one way to spell a word."

In all of this, remember that creativity, ingenuity, initiative, innovation, personalization, and application to your own life and circumstances are necessary.

Andrew Jackson jumped into greatness by boldly living in the storms that *he* encountered. By looking for the difference *he* could make in the world and truly making it. He fought *his* battles and achieved *his* victories. That's part of revolutionary leadership: Add to what's been done already by taking on the less-than-ideal parts of the status quo and never giving in to the human temptation to be mediocre.

Two Guiding Principles

Revolutionary leaders by definition do two things: they lead, and they revolutionize. So get to it!

Jump into greatness by facing your storms head on. Jump into greatness by living like there's no tomorrow. Be great right now, and fight like you have to, long before you actually do!

Jump into greatness by planning *and acting!* Don't let yourself be caught in endless planning, because leaders must also be *doers.*

Jump into greatness by being bold about what's right and also boldly righting your mistakes and wrongs.

Jump into greatness by being on the right side, no matter the personal cost. Jump into greatness by building a community of greatness around you.

And in all of this, don't forget to have fun innovating in ways that are better than anything the world has seen before! This is what it means to jump into greatness. By doing so, you're that much closer to being the right kind of leader, like Andrew Jackson was—a true revolutionary leader.

1910s–1930s: Associated with great minds on a regular basis and decided to become great himself. Moved to Germany, where he studied law and worked as an editor for one of Frankfurt's largest newspapers. Finished his Ph.D. in international law and fled to England to escape the Nazis, who had already burned some of his essays. Later, moved to the United States and taught economics part-time at Sarah Lawrence College in New York. Published his first book.

1940s–1950s: Launched his first consulting project, and served as professor of philosophy and politics at Bennington University. Became a naturalized citizen of the United States, wrote for The Wall Street Journal and Harper's Magazine, and published two more books. Started his official consulting firm, joined the University of New York Faculty, and published four more books.

1960s–2000s: Continued to rise in popularity as a speaker, professor, and consultant, and received awards and acclaim for his brilliant insight in the fields of management, leadership, and personal development. Published 32 more books.

4

PETER DRUCKER

Brush Up Your Greatness and Stop Being Un-Great!

P eter Drucker was one of the greatest minds in the leadership genre. In fact, he is often called the creator of the leadership/management revolution. He's considered a major forerunner of the fields of leadership and self-help.

Drucker was a powerful revolutionary, though not in the traditional sense. He did not "spit in the eye" of oppressive government, demand the freedom of his people from a tyrant, build a barricade and defend it with bullets and blood, or even draft a document telling the king that he would now be seen as an equal.

In fact, if he *had* done these things in the time and place he lived, it would have been far less impactful or meaningful than what he *did* accomplish.

Drucker was a revolutionary leader, not because he led battle charges or defended his flag through the night, but because he did what was his to do without holding back.

> **Peter Drucker saw the world and what it could and *should* be, and then he demanded—with everything he was and everything he did—that it move.**

Best-selling author Oliver DeMille defined a top level leader as "Someone who sees the world where it is, and where it should be, and then places himself in the middle—taking the steps he or she can to *bring* the world with him from where it is, toward where it should be." This is also a good definition of what it means to be a revolutionary leader.

> **The lessons that can be learned from this type of revolutionary innovation are deep and powerful. They are also nearly infinite in number and scope.**

Peter Drucker saw the world and what it could and *should* be, and then he demanded—with everything he was and everything he did—that it move.

And it did.

Real Change

When a true revolutionary stands with everything he has to offer, refuses to be less than great, and *requires* that the world be different—better—and actually succeeds, such leadership is undeniable, and the ensuing *revolution* is irreplaceable.

Peter Drucker spurred just such a revolution.

The lessons that can be learned from this type of revolutionary innovation are deep and powerful. They are also nearly infinite in number and scope.

Nevertheless, let us endeavor to explore just a few of the things that made Drucker great and have the power, when applied, to make other individuals more than simply observers of great change or revolution, but true revolutionary leaders in their own right.

"Knowledge has to be improved, challenged, and increased constantly, or it vanishes."

Peter grew up in Austria, and when he was a child, his family often hosted people for gatherings, parties, and intellectual discussions at their house. But not just any people. Some of the people he interacted with in his own home as a child included Joseph Schumpeter, F. A. Hayek, and Ludwig von Mises.

In short, he spent much of his childhood listening to and even participating in conversations with some of the greatest minds in history in the fields of economics, entrepreneurship, and leadership, night after night.

This is powerful! And of course, it led in large part to his success and brilliance in these areas, and his ability later in life to revolutionize the world of leadership.

Yet beyond this, interacting with them *did* something to him — it made him realize that he needed to read more and really catch up in the field of knowledge.

It became clear to him that if he wanted to be great, he couldn't afford to stay "un-great"! This may seem obvious, yet every leader in history who's been a part of a meaningful revolution and provided a significant contribution to society at some point or other had to sit down and decide to give up on being un-great. This is very important.

This decision is a turning point for any would-be leader. This usually means sacrificing certain pleasures, activities, and distractions, yet it is entirely worth it for those who truly dedicate their lives to a real life purpose and end up achieving the only kind of success that really matters — greatness at living your God-given life purpose to the fullest.

> **Think of the wide variety of broad and deep learning that would come from a lifestyle of digging for knowledge!**

Peter Drucker looked at those who were leading the world in powerful ways and living their purpose, and he knew he'd need to stop giving in to any temptation or weakness that led to less than greatness, stop being un-great in little things as well as big, and keep improving himself at every turn.

A Search

This sent him on a lifelong hunger and search for knowledge, wisdom, and understanding. He read, studied, and learned as much as he could for the rest of his life.

In fact, he made it a habit in his life to pick one new field or focus he'd never studied before every year, in which he had high interest and little knowledge. Then he would study it deeply for the whole year (in addition to the other important tasks in his life), discovering, learning, and internalizing as much as he could.

GREAT STRATEGY FOR LEARNING

Then the next year, he'd move to the next subject, then the next, and the next.

And this was on top of everything else he was already learning and accomplishing in his life, in addition to all of his other responsibilities and work, and in addition to even deeper learning in areas he had already mastered.

Drucker did this for his whole adult life, and he lived to be almost a hundred years old! Think of the wide variety of broad and deep learning that would come from such a lifestyle of digging for knowledge.

That's the type of life Drucker chose, and it determined the kind of man he became and the high level of influence and impact he was able to have on society and in the world.

> **Every leader in history who's been a part of a meaningful revolution and provided a significant contribution to society at some point or other had to sit down and decide to give up on being un-great.**

Because he was a lifelong seeker of the lessons, truth, and wisdom of the word, he ultimately became a powerful revolutionary leader in one of the most important ways: the revolutionary leader who comes in a time of peace and relative prosperity and *still* questions and takes on the status quo.

His lifelong battle against mediocrity is a powerful example. And it absolutely helped shift society toward increased leadership, ingenuity, prosperity, freedom, and overall progress. Even to *excellence*. This is a big deal.

This is the kind of leadership that genuinely *revolutionizes* the world, in a way that nothing else can.

Drink Deeply

Peter Drucker fell in love with learning and made a huge difference because of it. He loved to gain all sorts of knowledge, even studying authors and ideas that he disagreed with.

He studied them so deeply and so well that he could still disagree, but now he knew exactly why and how he disagreed and was able to approach the idea or topic with a full understanding that allowed him to really see the holes in things and truly solve problems in creative and effective ways.

This is fantastic training for revolutionary leadership. It teaches leaders how to see the things that need to change, how they need to be changed, and the best ways to implement change. They also learn how to gauge the overall effectiveness of changes made in the past, so they can start the process all over and fine-tune changes all the way to perfection.

This is commonly called the PDCA Process (Plan-Do-Check-Adjust), and it is one of the most powerful leadership tools and routines in the revolutionary leader's tool belt.

And as we learn from Peter Drucker, broad and deep study of all sorts of fields and authors, those you agree with and those you vehemently disagree with, is a fantastic way for top leaders to practice and even develop the skill of effectively and quickly PDCAing in their lives and the things they attempt.

In fact, PDCA is all about how to stop being un-great and how to improve upon your greatness! Peter Drucker teaches us how to learn this process to the point that it becomes our second nature.

How? Simple: start *using* it. Start actually doing with the things you're studying and learning, the things you're doing in work and career, the way you approach relationships, etc. Learn, analyze, improve. Over and over and over. This was one of Drucker's powerful contributions.

By improving, increasing, and challenging your knowledge, your skills, your wisdom, and your leadership, VERY and applying the PDCA process along the way, you'll GOOD be simultaneously cutting all ties to "un-greatness" and truly improve upon your greatness, which means you'll be building yourself as a powerful revolutionary leader.

1) DEFINE YOUR FUTURE
2) MAKE IT HAPPEN

"The best way to predict your future is to create it."

Another very important way to "improve upon your greatness" and stop being un-great is to start defining the future you want and begin making it happen.

Top leaders achieve success by defining what their own personal brand of success will look like, then going out and learning from those who have accomplished such success, and ultimately by actually getting down to business and doing the work that has always brought, and likely *will* always bring, true success.

> **This type of leadership is powerful and it can be summed up in a word: change.**

Drucker wanted to live in a future where things were drastically different—and significantly better—than the one he was born into. Not that the world wasn't good, but he knew it wasn't as good as it could be.

And when you're a visionary who sees how much better the world might be and how you can help make it that way, it's hard to sit around in the inferior world without taking steps to improve it. Especially for a revolutionary leader who has made the choice to stop being un-great.

So Drucker took his own advice and started creating the powerful and beautiful future he'd envisioned and wanted.

In his life he wrote 39 books and was well known to the point of fame in many groups around the world, and he was asked to speak in numerous venues.

But while he did speak often and in many places, his preference and his real *forte* was the behind-the-scenes leadership of going into companies that were struggling and helping them diagnose and change problem areas so they could really thrive and obtain their genuine purpose.

This type of leadership is powerful and it can be summed up in a word: change. In fact, "revolution" is another simple way to describe it.

Revolutionary leadership is *about* change—sometimes in big and obvious ways, but just as often, in the small and simple things that hold people and organizations back from performing and succeeding in the best ways.

Drucker understood the power and importance of change and dedicated his career and life to changing himself and helping others change in ways that really led to increased happiness, effectiveness, and success.

"Unless commitment is made, there are only promises and hopes."

In fact, because he was so committed to weeding out the bad in himself and truly building the great future he envisioned, he went well beyond the "hope" and "promise" phase and truly acted and shifted the world.

He actually spurred significant changes in thought and understanding in *several* fields and areas.

Ken Blanchard, one of the top people in the next generation of revolutionary leaders in the field of leadership and self-development—a generation largely inspired and even *brought on* by the efforts and impact of Drucker—said of him, "What I find is that, whenever I think I've got a really creative idea, if I go back to one of Peter's books, I always find he said it first!"

Follow His Example

Leaders can emulate Drucker by pushing future generations to go the extra mile and

> **Leaders don't lead by hope and promise alone.**

work hard to truly innovate, create, and *add* to what's been done before.

Revolutionary leaders like Drucker, and Franklin for that matter, are incredible examples because they're the kind of people who didn't make it easy for future generations to come up with original thoughts. Of course, they highly recommended original thinking; they just didn't leave many thoughts or ideas un-thought or un-discovered!

Another lesson: they never got to this point without true commitment. Leaders don't lead by hope and promise alone. They also lead through dedication, planning, acting, and continuously brushing up their greatness.

This is similar to what Stephen Covey referred to as "Sharpening the Saw" by doing the things that keep you strong and effective. Drucker's "improving upon greatness" adds to this the concept of always improving oneself. Or, in other words, sharpen your saw, and also utilize other and better tools in addition to your "saw "as you progress through life.

> **Leaders can emulate Drucker by pushing future generations to go the extra mile and work hard to truly innovate, create, and *add* to what's been done before.**

⭐ ***"If you want something new, you have to stop doing something old."*** ⭐

As we've already said, to become a great revolutionary leader, you have to do more than simply begin. You also have to let go of the "un-greatness" most people so often try to hold onto.

In order to start becoming the revolutionary leaders they hope to be—that new thing they want to become—prospective leaders must keep doing some of the old things that got them where they are and also really *stop* doing things that have held them back. This is the process of shedding the things about you and your habits that are "un-great".

It's just as important what a company, an organization, a family, a person, or a prospective revolutionary leader *doesn't* do as what it/he/she/they *do*. This matters deeply.

Drucker understood how important this was, and he applied it in his life and career. From the very beginning, when he decided he wanted to be educated and great like the guests in his childhood home, we see him consistently giving up un-greatness in order to become great.

The Parable of the Ham

Top leader Laurie Woodward shared the proverbial story of a young wife who sets out to cook a lovely meal for her new husband, so she picks out a great ham, cuts off the ends and sticks it in the oven.

When it's all done and she serves it to her husband, he loves it, but he's a bit confused. "Why is it that you cut the ends off? It seem like that's just a waste."

"No, no," she replies. "That's how you're supposed to do it — that's how my mom always did it."

On hearing this he nods. He really doesn't know much about cooking hams, and maybe they're right. Still, he doesn't see why he shouldn't have twice as much ham at the end of the day, so he pushes it a bit further.

"Maybe we should call your mom and ask her what that's all about — I'd really like to understand this whole thing."

The wife agrees, and they call her mother.

When the wife's mother answers the phone, they immediately ask her why it is that you're supposed to cut the ends off the ham, and she replies, simply, "Well, that's the way my mom always did it."

So they call up the grandma, and when they ask her why she cuts the ends of the ham, her answer shocks them all!

"Well, I did that because my pan was too small to fit the whole thing."

This story clearly illustrates how even things that are revolutionary and ingeniously innovative and creative for some people at a certain time aren't always the best or right things for new leaders facing new problems and seeking to create a new and better future.

It's important that those who seek to become revolutionary leaders follow the example and advice of Peter Drucker and stop doing the old things that no longer serve them.

After all, those things got them where they are, but to truly shift, change, improve, and *revolutionize* the world, leaders must stop doing old things that don't work and start coming up with new and inventive things that will take the world forward to its best future.

"There is nothing quite so useless, as doing with great efficiency, something that should not be done at all."

VERY GOOD

If Peter Drucker had decided to stop brushing up his greatness by dedicating all of his time to things that were quite frankly sub par, he wouldn't have achieved much that was worthy of our attention, admiration, or emulation.

However, when he chose to get a superb education and become a fantastic revolutionary leader, he also decided to stop being un-great. He then taught a lot of other people to do the same.

For example, when Jack Welch became CEO of General Electric, the company had been struggling. Welch immediately set up a meeting with Drucker to ask what they should be doing to get out of their rut and increase their effectiveness and success as a company.

Drucker told him that GE was so big, so disparate, and involved in so many fields that, even if it had made sense at one time to be in this or that field, it didn't make sense anymore. Yet the company was still doing it.

Drucker told him right off the bat that they'd be better off to focus first on what they *shouldn't* be doing. That said, Drucker also suggested that it was just as important to keep doing the things that they really *should* be doing! In other words, you have to have both sides: brush up your greatness *and* stop being un-great!

People who hope to become revolutionary leaders can learn from Peter Drucker to ask the important questions in all their spheres of influence and leadership, from personal to family, from business to community, and beyond.

In harmony with this principle, one business leader taught that those who hope to really increase their effectiveness and more fully dedicate themselves to their purpose in life should ask themselves the following questions:

Do THIS

*1. What are the top five things I need to accomplish in the next six months in my business/family/community/etc. in order to really further my life purpose and get me closer to my dreams in life?

* 2. What are the top five things I spend my time on each day?

Answering these two questions allows leaders to clearly track their effectiveness and whether or not they're spending time on the things that really matter. To take it a step further, we suggest also asking the following questions:

> **Peter Drucker achieved incredible success simply by being willing to stop doing the things that didn't matter and start doing the things that did.**

1. Are the things I'm spending my time on relevant to the things I hope to accomplish?

2. Are the things I do still as valid as they were when I first started doing them?

3. Is there anything I'm spending my time on that is actually distracting me from my purpose and holding me back from success?

4. What am I doing that would qualify as "un-great"?

5. What things can I stop doing without negative consequences?

6. What can I do to replace the old, "un-great" things I used to do with innovative things that will lead to real improvement?

7. How can I brush up my greatness?

Once you have the answers to all of these questions, go to work implementing the things you've learned. Throughout his life, Peter Drucker achieved incredible success simply by being willing to stop doing the things that didn't matter and start doing the things that did. This is so simple, but it's so important.

WHY NOT

This is what it means to brush up your greatness and stop being un-great, and it's a vital piece of revolutionary leadership.

"The purpose of business is to create and keep a customer."

Another powerful aspect of both brushing up your greatness and stopping the un-great, is serving people. Anyone who hopes to be a truly powerful revolutionary leader must take care of the people they serve and lead.

Peter Drucker is an excellent example of servant leadership. His whole career was dedicated to teaching the principles that make a happy and successful life and business and helping people learn and apply them in their own families and careers.

He mentored company after company and leader after leader, helping people solve their problems and achieve their hopes, dreams, and goals.

This matters so much!

When it comes to leadership, the first and most important thing for anyone to do is *serve.*

Orrin Woodward said, "The more you serve, the more you deserve."

Peter Drucker taught and lived by the principle that in order to be genuinely effective and truly great, a leader must forget about the credit, the rewards, and the personal benefits and must focus instead on serving, helping and benefitting others, and on the difference he or she can make in the world.

> **When it comes to leadership, the first and most important thing for anyone to do is *serve.***

Revolutionary leaders achieve the height of their success by helping followers, mentees, protégés, and others benefit from their service, be inspired by their excellence, and carry on their legacy of revolutionary leadership long after they are gone.

This is what brings true success to revolutionary leaders, and it is also the best way to be a truly excellent person.

"Whenever you see a successful business, someone once made a courageous decision."

We've said it before, but it bears repeating: In order to brush up your greatness and stop being un-great, you have to make the choice, and that's going to take a fair amount of courage. This is true now, and also at every step on the path of leadership.

Drucker faced many challenges throughout his life, and he received a lot of criticism and experienced a lot of pain in the process. Nevertheless, he decided to be great, he decided to be courageous, and he kept at it.

He decided that being a little boy who listened with bright eyes to the brilliance of others wasn't enough for him. So he made a courageous decision.

He committed to a life of passionate learning. This led him to all sorts of important knowledge and wisdom.

He showed the courage to define and create his own bright future. He moved beyond hopes and promises and truly *committed* to his dreams and their success.

This led him to the actions that made all the difference in his ability to *make* a significant difference in the world! It also helped him come up with many deep and original thoughts that created a powerful legacy for those who followed him.

He repeatedly emphasized putting your energy into the things that truly matter and doing them *right. And he dedicated his life to advocating the importance of true servant-leadership.*

His works inspired a generation of others to apply his messages of truly excellent leadership. All of this because he made the decisions that truly counted and *chose* to be a revolutionary leader!

1942: Joined the military, in the United States Army Intelligence Corps.

1945: Left the army and took over a Ben Franklin's Five and Dime variety store franchise. Built it into a successful enterprise and industry leader.

1950: Lost his first store and started over from scratch.

1950–62: Built his Ben Franklin's chain into the biggest operation of variety stores in the Southwest.

1962: Opened the first Wal-Mart. Built it into a global leader over the next two decades.

1985: Was named the richest man in the United States.

1992: Received the Presidential Medal of Freedom.

OBSESSED
FANATICAL

"To have long-term success…in any position of leadership, you have to be obsessed in some way."
—PAT RILEY

5

SAM WALTON

Expect Greatness

1) BIG DREAM
2) WILLINGNESS TO WORK HARD
3) COMPETITIVE DETERMINATION TO WIN

Sam Walton, like Peter Drucker, was a revolutionary leader who specialized, not in ending some crisis during a major societal downturn, but in taking the opportunity and freedom provided by societal and economic highs to inspire and lead the world to a higher level.

He started out with no connections and seemingly everything working against him. However, he had a big dream, a willingness to work hard, and a competitive determination to win every time.

Because of this, Walton made the leadership world a different place, achieved wild success, beat odds that were undeniably against him, and revolutionized the way business is done in the world.

Doing this in and of itself is enough to rank him among the lists of great revolutionary leaders. Interestingly, though, he actually did it all specifically by revolutionizing the way leadership was approached in business.

He totally shifted the way that people saw positions and interactions within a corporate hierarchy, and he made it so that leadership was something you see not just at the top of a business but throughout it, at every level. He made leadership an essential part of top-to-bottom organizational behavior.

Sam Walton expected greatness of himself, and he truly achieved it. But what made him even *greater*, the reason we still talk about him today, and the reason he's in this book, is that he also invited and expected greatness from others—in fact, from everyone within the organization!

> He loved to offer people the opportunity to become great leaders by giving them the responsibility and the support that would naturally incentivize great results.

> Sam Walton expected greatness of himself, and he truly achieved it.

He came from "nowhere" and built himself to greatness by being willing to commit to something that mattered to him, and then stick it out no matter the difficulties. Because he was a "nobody" who became great, he couldn't deny the potential of anyone to come from whatever background and achieve success and greatness, and to truly change the world.

He knew it was possible because he'd done it himself. And he never forgot it.

The Power of Attitude ✳

1) WORK
2) SACRIFICE
3) STRUGGLE
4) GROWTH

Perhaps Walton's greatest success came from the attitude that anyone can be great, but that doing so will take ¹work, ²sacrifice, ³struggle, and ⁴growth before the final victory.

He built a culture of leadership and greatness by truly inviting and even *expecting* others to be willing to pay the price of greatness, in order to obtain the rewards. He loved to offer people the opportunity to become great leaders by giving them the ¹responsibility and the ²support that would naturally incentivize great results.

He believed in people, he encouraged people, and he expected them to beat the odds and truly impress and amaze the world. Because of this, many of them actually did!

> **"If you're going to be a winner, you've got to hate losing!"** ✵

With all of that said, let's jump into some of the specific things that made him different from anyone and everyone else — the things that made him great. Let's see what helped make Sam Walton such a truly revolutionary leader.

"High expectations are the key to everything."

As we've already mentioned, Sam Walton started out with no connections, but he had a big dream and a willingness to work. He also had a hugely competitive nature.

In his four years of high school, he never once lost a football game — not once! Very few people can boast such a thing, and that doesn't necessarily mean they're destined to fall short of Walton's achievements in life, but it does show something incredible about the character of Sam Walton.

He said himself that by all rights he should have lost some games at some point along the way, but they always managed to pull it together at the last minute. Of course, one of the main reasons for this, as his teammates said, was that Sam Walton hated to lose!

Not only was he unwilling to lose, but he inspired the same passion in his teammates. Because of this, he consistently paid the price to be a winner.

Orrin Woodward teaches that "If you're going to be a winner, you've got to hate losing!" Sam Walton truly exemplified this zero-tolerance stance toward losing, and it helped him become an incredible winner.

This is one of the things that make a revolutionary leader what he or she is — hating to lose and being willing to change. And as Woodward put it, winners "hate losing *enough* to change!"

Walton started expecting greatness by applying this directly to himself. He didn't want to lose, so instead he *changed*.

Breaking the Right Rules

In his book *Giants of Enterprise,* Richard S. Tedlow said of Sam Walton: "First he learned all the rules, then he broke all the rules which did not make sense to him, which meant almost all of them."

Since he knew he didn't want to lose, and that meant he'd need to change, Walton set some pretty high expectations for himself. This meant that he had to break any of the hard and fast "rules" of what he could or couldn't become, what he was or wasn't good at, and what he could or couldn't accomplish.

Any of the limiting beliefs or weaknesses he saw in himself that most people might have been tempted to call "rules," or simply, "the way things are," Sam Walton saw as the potential to lose—problems to be blasted away so he could *do* what he needed, to *be* who he wanted to be, and to *get* what he wanted in life!

> **This is one of the things that make a revolutionary leader what he or she is—hating to lose and being willing to change.**

"I have always been driven to buck the system, to innovate, to take things beyond where they've been."

Sam Walton got his start, as a very young man, when the Butler brothers gave him the management of their worst, most struggling, least profitable Franklin's Five and Dime store.

At the time, *they* didn't even think he'd be able to make it work; they just wanted to see what he could do with it.

Expecting nothing less than greatness, and completely defying their expectations, Sam Walton did more than simply "make it work." In fact, through his hard work and innovations, in five years he turned the store into the most profitable one in the whole chain.

During this process, Walton found that the Butler brothers' tight controls and strict regulations made it difficult for him to really serve his customers.

> **Sam Walton continued to learn and grow, expecting and demanding greatness of himself, and learning to help and inspire others to do the same.**

Very early on, he started looking for ways to get around the rules by finding less-expensive suppliers, ignoring many of the more expensive items proposed by the Butler brothers, and attempting to lower prices to more fully satisfy customers. He really did "buck the system!" And he did it the *right* way by innovating and really taking things far beyond how they'd been done before.

If we ask who Walton was focused on, himself or his customer, the answer is pretty clear: his first priority as a businessman was to please his customers.

Walton understood that to be successful in any type of business, the first step is and *has to be* to satisfy the customer. His approach was simple: find out what the customer needs and wants and give it to him on a consistent basis.

That was Sam Walton's first step, and it led to quite a bit of success in the long term.

For his first few years in business he saw huge success in his little five and dime store, with 45 percent growth the first year, an additional 33 percent the second, and 25 percent on top of that the third year. He

> **His first priority as a businessman was to please his customers.**

literally went from worst to first in a few short years by learning to expect greatness from himself and his own company right from the get-go, by putting "first things first" and by consistently taking care of his customers.

The Power of Setbacks — WILLIE JOLEY

What happened next seemed like a huge wrench thrown into his plans, but it led to even greater success as Sam Walton continued to learn and grow, expecting and demanding greatness of himself, and learning to help and inspire others to do the same.

After five years of successfully building his business, Sam Walton lost the store.

Unfortunately, when he first started out, he was young and more bright-eyed and enthusiastic than careful or detail-oriented, and when he signed the lease for the building that housed his store, he hadn't really looked into it or made sure it included all the important details. At that point, he may not have even known exactly what to look for in a contract.

Specifically, he hadn't checked for any provisions for renewing the lease before it expired. Even though such a provision was practically standard in store leases, the lease he'd signed didn't have it. And when the lease ended, the building owner saw it as a chance to make Walton sell off all the merchandise cheaply, setting up his own son to make easy money off the success that Sam Walton had spent the last five years building.

Walton lost the store, had to sell everything for a mere $50,000 — much less than it was worth — and cut his losses. He'd have to start over a new franchise of the same Franklin's Five and Dime and build it all over again from the bottom.

With the $50,000 from selling his other store, he'd have almost enough to start a store that was only half the size of what he'd had before. This hurt.

Speaking of the experience, Walton said: "This was the low point of my life. I felt sick to my stomach. I couldn't believe it was happening to me — it was really like a nightmare. I had built the best variety store in the whole region, and worked hard in the community — done everything right! And now I was being kicked out of town. It didn't seem fair.

"I blamed myself for getting suckered into such an awful lease, and I was furious with the landlord. Helen was just settling in with a brand new family of four, and was heartsick at the prospect of leaving Newport. But that's what we were going to do."

It's powerful to see how, though like the rest of humanity he couldn't control the cards he was dealt, Sam Walton was determined to control how he played them. ✯ ✯

He experienced huge opposition and even failure, yet he knew that he could be great and he expected himself to act like it. Because of this, he didn't give up when it seemed so obvious that he should. Instead, he stood up and kept going.

"I had to pick myself up and get on with it, do it all over again, only even better this time."

Instead of crying over dashed expectations or bemoaning how the world had treated him, he raised his expectations for himself and determined to become even greater. He turned difficulties in the direction of improvement. He decided to build an even better business this time.

Walton learned from this experience and revolutionized his own approach in some pretty significant ways because of it.

First of all, he hired an excellent legal team and never again signed a contract without having it thoroughly looked into and making sure it wasn't going to cause problems for him in the future.

Another thing that he did, which was really important and helped set him up for future success and excellence, was that he didn't pass the buck. He took full responsibility for his situation and the things he did that put him there. In this way he was expecting greatness from himself and recognizing when and where he fell short, which allowed him to learn, change, grow, and become even more successful.

> **He refused to pass the buck or play the victim card, even when doing so seemed very alluring.**

He refused to pass the buck or play the victim card, even when doing so seemed very alluring. Instead, he allowed the pain of these temporary setbacks to fuel the fire of his future growth!

Starting Better

Walton bought and set up his much smaller franchise in Bentonville, Arkansas, and for the next twelve years, from 1950 to 1962, he worked hard to expand his operations to a much higher level, ultimately becoming the man behind the largest independent variety store operation around. He just kept building store after store after store.

And this was still pre-Wal-Mart! This was all accomplished while building Franklin's Five and Dime stores. Walton was expanding the Butler brothers' business, making them richer and richer, before he had even branched out and created his own real *life work*.

When you combine this with the five years he worked on his first store, Sam Walton spent seventeen years of his life building a business that wasn't even his own! But all of this was the preparation he'd need to make Wal-Mart what it became.   *EXCELLENT*

These years were an investment in himself.

Walton worked very hard and became very good at what he did, so that in 1962, when he started his first Wal-Mart, even though he didn't have the backing of billionaires or the popularity or acclaim that his competitors enjoyed, he was able to build it to a level that ultimately left the others far back in the dust.

"Outstanding leaders go out of their way to boost the self-esteem of their personnel."

When he started Wal-Mart, there were actually three other companies—all of which are familiar names today — launching as discount stores at the same time. And Wal-Mart was seen as the smallest and most under-capitalized. Most people thought that it had the least chance of making it.

Yet a few decades later, you could add all the rest of those companies together, plus a few more on the side, and Wal-Mart far exceeded them all in competition and success!

This is because Sam Walton created a leadership culture. And this isn't a matter of 10 percent or even 20 percent better results; we're talking magnitudes of tens, and hundreds, and literally thousands of times more success than some of his early competitors.

Creating a culture of widespread leadership throughout his organization as Sam Walton did, and an expectation of greatness, is truly powerful. And it generally revolutionizes the industry one is working in, because one ends up with a whole field of revolutionary leaders who choose and expect greatness and great leadership.

Orrin Woodward teaches that a leadership culture is the number one competitive advantage that any company can have over its competitors. He said: "Any technology that you come up with, your competitor will have it in just a matter of time — mostly within weeks! Any super plan you have, they can copy your plan. But you know what they can't copy? Do you know what's nearly *impossible* to copy? Your leadership culture."

This is the main and best competitive advantage possible, and this is how Sam Walton was able to produce the results he did. He revolutionized business because he set up a leadership culture. He was able to create that culture because he was willing and determined to be the best leader he could be, in a way that he didn't need to be *the* leader!

Instead of being threatened by other leaders, he encouraged them, invested in them, searched them out, and *expected* them to rise up and be great. This was the crux of his whole business model.

Walton was an outstanding leader, by his own definition and by ours, because he not only believed in people, he not only inspired people — he truly *expected* that a whole bunch of them would want to be great to the point that they'd be willing to do the work of true leadership.

And then he set up an effective system to help incentivize, build, develop, and reward them for meeting his expectation of their greatness — and holding themselves to an even higher standard.

"If people believe in themselves, it's amazing what they can accomplish."

VERY TRUE !!

Walton had a special approach to doing business — a revolutionary leadership style that led a lot of other people to powerful leadership. He believed in people so much, and expected so much from them, that many of them really met his expectations. Of course, communication was critical in all of this.

It's not enough to merely believe in the ability of others to be great revolutionary leaders. To achieve real success, one must also get them to want it, and then help them come to believe it is possible, and then to *expect* it of themselves.

This is what Sam Walton did, and he did it by adding to everything else we've discussed — the power of "communicate, communicate, communicate."

He said, "The necessity for good communication in a big company like this is so vital that it cannot be overstated." This is pretty obvious in a situation like Wal-Mart, since it was so vast and always growing that there was no way that Sam Walton could call up every store each day and talk to them and see how they were doing.

But he knew the importance of communication, so he decided to set a high bar of greatness for himself, his company, his leaders, his organization, his associates, and so on, and he knew they could somehow find a way to make it work. Specifically, in addition to all the daily internal communications, he created a special Saturday meeting that involved all the stores and leaders throughout the whole chain of Wal-Marts across the world, so they could experience the kind of communication needed to continue to grow and achieve the level of success Sam Walton envisioned for his people.

> **Communication of vision, belief, and the expectation of greatness among all those you lead or influence is a vital part of revolutionary leadership in any sphere or aspect of society.**

Even though he couldn't meet with every individual in his company, every day, to discuss every topic, he established a system so that every Saturday the stores would be able to hear his voice and his thoughts. He'd be able to share his insights and suggestions and *cast a vision* for where the company needed to go.

This process helped him inspect the successes and failures, progress and obstacles, needs and problems in the company, and it also gave him the chance to help fix such issues, strengthen his leaders, articulate his expectations, build the belief of everyone involved, and continue to help develop leaders throughout the company.

Communication of vision, belief, and the expectation of greatness among all those you lead or influence is a vital part of revolutionary leadership in any sphere or aspect of society. By getting this right, those who seek to be true revolutionary leaders will find that their leadership works better and their revolution goes further.

This matters so much, and it makes such an incredible difference.

> **"The more you share profits with your associates, whether it's in salaries, or incentives, or bonuses, or stock discounts, the more profit will accrue to the company."**

In addition, the number one factor in the success of Wal-Mart may well be Sam Walton's completely revolutionary profit-sharing model. He created a business model by which the people who ran each store had the chance to benefit from it as if it was their own store! And they'd benefit based on the success or failure of their own individual work and leadership in their location.

Walton really set up a culture of leaders. He innovatively established a situation that attracted and rewarded leaders for standing up and being excellent, innovative, creative, and effective.

These rewards weren't based on who they knew or how well they played the game or knew the ropes. Their rewards were based on how well they performed as individuals and as teams. Success was based on how well they developed and proved themselves as leaders.

Anyone and everyone had the chance to become a leader and to achieve incredible success in this system — in fact they were *expected* to. This is powerful!

Because he did it this way, because he gave the opportunity to everyone to rise up and be great and get the rewards associated with success if they were willing to pay the price and live up to the responsibilities involved, he was truly inviting, challenging, and *expecting* other people to become absolutely phenomenal performers and real revolutionary leaders.

Sam Walton watched for and incentivized greatness at every turn, and in such a way that it actually made a difference in people's lives so that they really *did* become great. This type of win/win thinking genuinely invited greatness from anyone and everyone and is what made Wal-Mart great.

Sharing Greatness

Expecting greatness of others means getting excited to *share* greatness with those who are willing to truly obtain it. When individuals know that they have a chance to significantly benefit from and share in the profit that comes from real greatness and genuine revolutionary leadership, more and more will be willing to take on the work and sacrifice required to get there.

By giving people a level of *ownership*, credit and responsibility for success or failure, leaders have a much better chance of building and developing *other* leaders! Chris Brady and Orrin Woodward called this "launching a leadership revolution," in their excellent book by this title. In the end, everyone benefits more, as the world undergoes a huge revolutionary shift!

> **Today, more than ever, we need more and more leaders of the caliber of Sam Walton.**

Sam Walton understood that in business, it's all about treating your people right. Leaders have to learn to take care of their people on every level. If owners treat associates right, associates are more likely to treat customers right. And if associates and customers feel fabulously taken care of, the company will flourish, grow, progress, and achieve real and lasting success.

Interestingly, the three other big discount store companies that came out in 1962 were K Mart, WoolCo, and Target. All of them were backed by big capital, and all had very promising and acclaimed business plans and people spearheading them.

Yet today, Wal-Mart is without question the most successful of the bunch, even though Sam Walton—not a billionaire at the time—could find almost no one to invest in him or support his cause, and he had to come up with 95 percent of the original investment himself.

The reason for this success was his brilliant revolutionary leadership, the level of communication he built into the company, and the leadership culture he created: to expect greatness and to provide leaders the opportunity to become great themselves.

The very fact that he didn't start highly wealthy contributed in large part to his success, since it led him to create a team-like environment from day one. And the record shows pretty clearly what the results have been. Sam Walton won.

Go and Emulate

Today, more than ever, we need more and more leaders of the caliber of Sam Walton: Revolutionary leaders who are willing to expect greatness of themselves, even during lean or hard times, and make it to victory.

> **The world needs *you* to be a leader who is willing to play the game to win, by *expecting* greatness!**

We need more leaders who expect greatness by standing up and doing *even better*, anytime they get knocked down!

It's time to start expecting greatness by not settling for the results of current systems or conventions—to buck them off and do things in ways they've never been done before, *better* ways!

The world needs revolutionary leaders who are willing to expect greatness in others to the point that they really *do* develop greatness, which in turn develops other leaders who are willing to give up being credited as "the guy" or "the gal," and instead create a leadership culture full of people who *could* be the guy or the gal if they got the call.

The world needs revolutionary leaders who are willing to expect greatness from their organizations and in their circle of influence, so much so that they constantly look at the scoreboard, make improvements and changes as needed, and are consistently growing and progressing and becoming *greater!*

As we learn from the example and teachings of Sam Walton, the world needs *you* to be a leader who is willing to play the game to win, by *expecting* greatness!

CONCLUSION

"In a time not distant, it will possible to flash any image formed in thought on a screen and render it visible at any place desired."
—NIKOLA TESLA

"Leaders must be close enough to relate to others, but far enough ahead to motivate them."
—JOHN C. MAXWELL

Interestingly enough, there are people in the world today who believe that we are now at an all-time low for humanity — that immorality, suffering, environmental degradation, and the force exerted by technologically empowered governments across the globe are creating an era of increasingly drastic problems.

On the other hand, some people believe that the rapid increase of technological advancements in our time is the forerunner of a new epoch of great peace, economic prosperity, and personal freedoms — a period of human success like none ever before experienced in human history.

Between these two extremes, still other people feel that the leading powers of North America and Europe are beginning an era of significant economic, political, and moral decline. Yet others argue that we will see greatly increased prosperity in the Age of the Internet and that good times are just ahead.

Whatever ends up being true (one of these four, or some other view), one thing is very clear: the need in the world for real visionaries, rascals who buck the norm, and genuine, dedicated revolutionary leaders is as strong as ever.

There are so many things that need to be changed — in every nation, and in nearly all communities and sectors of society. We are a world, and a people, with so much potential, but so many serious challenges.

It is as true now as it ever has been that leadership is pivotal to the achievement, success, and progress of society and the world. And revolutionary leadership is one of the greatest and most impactful assets in any society.

A lack of revolutionary leadership means that a lot of important and good things won't happen.

The world needs a huge rise in leadership and greatness. Best-selling authors Chris Brady and Orrin Woodward called for this very kind of major change in the business world in their book *Launching a Leadership Revolution,* and Orrin Woodward and Oliver DeMille outlined the need for the same thing in the civic and political world in their best-selling book *LeaderShift.*

> **The world truly needs bold and courageous visionaries and genuine revolutionary leaders to step out of the realm of comfort and convention and make the difference in the world that only they can!**

The book you are reading right now adds to these by showing how five great revolutionary leaders made a huge, lasting difference in the word by applying these principles. We can learn so much from their examples. They have so much to teach us. We need to internalize and implement the lessons they left for us.

We need to build on their shoulders and take action. Leadership action.

Take Courage

True revolutionary leaders today must become more than mere dreamers, creative thinkers, "smart people," or simply individuals with good ideas. They must become the next generation of truly great leadership revolutionaries by being willing to think, innovate, and create not just in their heads but out loud, for everyone to hear, witness, and emulate.

The world truly needs bold and courageous visionaries and genuine revolutionary leaders to step out of the realm of comfort and convention and make the difference in the world that only they can!

We invite you to learn from the great revolutionary leaders discussed in this book and to rise to such leadership yourself.

Defying the societal norm and being willing to change yourself enough to change the world along with you is precisely what is needed to be a revolutionary leader. This means more than merely knowing what the world needs and dabbling at making it happen.

It is time for more of us to go "all in" for greatness and success in our life purpose, in our daily work and service, and in the way we build leaders in our homes, businesses, and communities.

We've discussed many things in this book that can lead to greatness and great revolutionary leadership. In order to be a truly effective revolutionary leader, it is very helpful to internalize, apply, and live by the principles that have always made the difference between those who simply hope to be better than average and those leaders who genuinely make the world a better place.

More Lessons

Such qualities include the many already covered in this book, and also the following additional lessons:

1. Focus on greatness long enough and well enough to get through hard times and create real victory.
2. When you do stumble, fall or get knocked down, stand up and make yourself even better!
3. Don't settle for the way things are when they aren't working or when you could make them better.
4. Learn to *develop* other great leaders, who develop even more leaders.
5. Be willing to give up the credit or the acclaim at times in order to help build other leaders.
6. Create a leadership culture full of people who *can* be top leaders when they get the opportunity.

7. Watch the scoreboard and make improvements and changes as needed, so you're consistently growing and progressing.

8. Decide to be great. Make a plan, and get to work on it. Take courage and keep at it!

9. Commit to a life of continual learning. Read, read, read. Listen to effective leadership audios and other important audios. Engage excellent workshops, trainings, and other opportunities to learn.

10. Define and create your own bright future.

11. Take your vision beyond hopes and promises and truly *commit* to your dreams and success. Do the hard work necessary for you to be great.

What kind of revolutionary will you be?

12. Know when it is time to throw out the old to make room for the new, and do it wisely and innovatively.

13. Focus your energy on the things that truly matter, and make sure you're doing them *right.*

14. Face your storms head on.

15. Live like there's no tomorrow — be great right *now,* and fight like you have to, long before you actually do!

16. Plan *and act!* Don't let yourself be caught in endless planning — revolutionary leaders must also be *doers.*

17. But do make good plans. Then implement them.

18. Be bold about what's right and also boldly "make right" your mistakes and wrongs.

19. Be on the right side, no matter the personal cost. This is when revolutions really matter.

20. Build teams and a community of greatness around you. Serve your community.

21. Have fun innovating ways that are simply better than anything the world has seen before! Start with the hard work of doing what you really should be doing right now.

22. Invite everyone to join the battle, whether they seem like the perfect candidate or not.

23. Be willing to learn the truth—the good, the bad, and the ugly. And then act on it accordingly and wisely.

24. Be bold enough to stand for right, even when it's hard or nearly impossible.

25. Carve out minutes in your already busy life to invest in greatness, and dedicate the time you already have to greatness by connecting your minutes in a way that will lead to a better you. Make sure your hours are spent on the right things.

26. Live the next month and year of your life in a way that will leave you more free to answer when the calls to be great come to you.

27. Remember that becoming a great revolutionary leader really will take time—it's not going to happen all at once, so be patient with your-

What is the world waiting for from you, and how can you rise to the challenge?

self and just keep improving every minute, every hour, every day, every week.

28. As you're being patient with your growth, make sure you're still doing the right things that will *make* you great.

29. Start now. Right now...

Make it a Revolution

And along with all these things, ask yourself the following questions: What can you be best a How can you make it a revolution? What kind of revolutionary will you be?

Once you've answered these questions, go and *become* such a leader.

What is the world waiting for from you, and how can you rise to the challenge? How can you team up with the greatest men and women from history by learning the lessons they taught and beat the expectations of those who haven't yet realized how much they need your leadership?

Do it.

Were you born to be a Franklin or a Henry? Were you born to be a Jackson? Were you born to be a Peter Drucker or a Sam Walton?

Who were you born to be?

The lessons from great leaders of the past are relevant today. The lives, works, and teachings of Benjamin Franklin, Patrick Henry, Andrew Jackson, Peter Drucker, Sam Walton, and other great leaders are still applicable.

As we apply the lessons they taught, we can rise to higher levels of leadership ourselves.

One thing is certain: you were born for an important life purpose. You can make yourself matter. The world has you in it for a reason.

So what's your revolution to fight? What is your brand of revolutionary leadership?

Find out. Write it down. Think about it every hour. And go out and live it. Out loud.

That's revolutionary.

That's leadership.

And that's *you*, and the focus of *your* greatest life, if you choose to accept your calling to be a leader, a rascal, a dreamer, and a doer. *Your* best life is as a revolutionary leader, and now is the time to get started.

> **One thing is certain: you were born for an important life purpose.**

It's time to act. Remember, as basketball great Larry Bird put it, "Leadership is diving for the loose ball." What is the "loose ball" in your life? The great thing you can do so much better — that will make *all* the difference for your future?

Now is the time to dive...

FINANCIAL FITNESS PROGRAM

Get Out of Debt and Stay Out of Debt!

FREE PERSONAL WEBSITE

SIGN UP AND TAKE ADVANTAGE OF THESE FREE FEATURES:

- Personal website
- Take your custom assessment test
- Build your own profile
- Share milestones and successes with partners and friends
- Post videos and photos
- Receive daily info "nuggets"

FINANCIAL FITNESS BASIC PROGRAM

The first program to teach all three aspects of personal finance: defense, offense, and playing field. Learn the simple, easy-to-apply principles that can help you shore up your resources, get out of debt, and build stability for a more secure future. It's all here, including a comprehensive book, companion workbook, and 8 audios that amplify the teachings from the books.

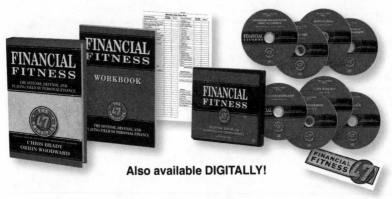

Also available DIGITALLY!

financialfitnessinfo.com

FINANCIAL FITNESS
MASTER CLASS

Buy it once and use it forever! Designed
to provide a continual follow-up to the
principles learned in the Basic Program,
this ongoing educational support offers over
6 hours of video and over 14 hours of audio
instruction that walk you through the workbook, step by step.
Perfect for individual or group study.
6 videos, 15 audios

FINANCIAL FITNESS
TRACK AND SAVE

The Financial Fitness Program teaches
you how to get out of debt, build additional
streams of income, and properly take
advantage of tax deductions. Now, with this
subscription, we give you the tools to do so. The
Tracker offers mobile expense tracking tools and budgeting software,
while the Saver offers you thousands of coupons and discounts to
help you save money every day.

WEALTH HABITS SERIES

Subscribe to the Wealth Habits Series and enjoy it on it's own, or use it as a supplement to enhance the existing suite of Financial Fitness Products. On a monthly basis, subscribers will learn to consistently apply the habits taught in the Financial Fitness Program in order to achieve financial goals and create long-term, sustainable wealth. Don't miss your chance to build top-notch wealth habits!

WEALTHABITS
SERIES

Physical Product Details:
- Month 1 - 3 audio inaugural pack and quality carrying case
- Month 2 and each month thereafter – 1 audio

Digital Product Details:
- Month 1 – 3 digital downloads
- Month 2 and each month thereafter – 1 digital download

S